النور المبين
في قواعد عقائد الدين

The Clear Light
Fundamentals of Religious Beliefs

Imām Muḥammad ibn Aḥmad ibn Muḥammad ibn Juzayy
Al-Kalbī Al-Gharnāṭī Al-Mālikī

(d. 741 AH)

Translated by
Fahim Hoosen

Contents

Translator's Preface

When I received the book, *Al-Nūr Al-Mubīn*, for the first time in 2015, I had just about completed the translation and commentary on the section of *Kitāb al-Buyū*ʿ (Book of Commercial Transactions) from the *Mukhtaṣar al-Qudūri*. The clarity and lucid presentation of the evidences for religious beliefs wholly supported by Qurʾānic texts immediately prompted me to proceed with using this book for teaching purposes at Madrasa Ḥamīdiyya in Durban, South Africa. Thereafter, I decided to translate it for the benefit of English readers.

When translating the Arabic text, I have attempted to remain as close to the source as possible, so as to preserve the author's originality and method of presentation.

The Arabic edition of the book contains copious excerpts from Ibn Juzayy's exegesis of the Qurʾān, titled *Al-Tashīl li Ulūm al-Tanzīl* in the footnotes. These were omitted in the translation. Instead a few footnotes were added by the translator wherever needed. Where Ibn Juzayy makes reference to Qurʾānic verses without quoting the full verse in the book, the full text of such verses was quoted in the footnotes, where necessary, to make it easy for the reader to refer to. In addition, the chapter and verse reference for all Qurʾānic quotations were included in the footnotes so the reader can easily refer directly to the Qurʾān and its commentaries if so required.

For the translation of Qurʾānic verses, the translation by MAS Abdel Haleem was mainly relied on with a few amendments wherever deemed appropriate by the translator, especially to translate the verse in accordance with the interpretation adduced by the author.

May Allah grant us the true understanding of religion and enable us to apply it correctly.

Fahim Hoosen
Durban, South Africa
January 2017 / Rabīʿ Al-Thānī 1438

Note on Transliteration

The transliteration of Arabic words generally follows the International Journal of Middle East Studies (IJMES) system with the use of *aw* and *ay* for diphthongs instead of *au* and *ai*.

Diacritical dots are used to mark the emphatic consonants (ط-ظ-ص-ض) as well as (ح): ṭ-ẓ-ṣ-ḍ-ḥ.

The Arabic letters (ث-ذ-خ-ش-غ) are represented in Latin letters with the familiar simplified spelling *th, dh, kh, sh* and *gh.*

The Arabic *tāʾ marbūṭa* is rendered *a* not *ah.*

The *nisba* ending is rendered *-iyya* in Arabic (e.g., *miṣriyya*).

The initial *hamza* is always dropped.

The definite article *al-* is lowercase everywhere, except when the first word of a sentence.

Please refer to the transliteration key on the next page for quick reference.

Transliteration Key

ا	*ā*	ط	*ṭ*
ب	*b*	ظ	*ẓ*
ت	*t*	ع	ʿ
ث	*th*	غ	*gh*
ج	*j*	ف	*f*
ح	*ḥ*	ق	*q*
خ	*kh*	ك	*k*
د	*d*	ل	*l*
ذ	*dh*	م	*m*
ر	*r*	ن	*n*
ز	*z*	ه	*h*
س	*s*	و	*w, aw, ū*
ش	*sh*	ي	*y, ay, ī*
ص	*ṣ*	ء	ʾ
ض	*ḍ*		

Imām Ibn Juzayy

Muḥammad bin Aḥmad bin Muḥammad bin Juzayy Al-Kalbī, whose agnomen was Abū l-Qāsim, was from Spanish Andalusia, and was from a family of prestige and nobility. He was born in the year 693 AH, in a city of learning and knowledge in that era, Granada.

He was dedicated to the pursuit of religious knowledge and occupied with learning, teaching and writing in various disciplines such as Arabic, legal theory, Qur'ānic recitations, prophetic traditions, literature, Qur'ānic exegesis. He was appointed to deliver the Friday sermon at the Grand Mosque of Granada at a young age.

Amongst his teachers were Abū Ja'far ibn Al-Zubayr (d. 708 AH), Ibn al-Kammād (d. 712 AH), Ibn Rushayd (d. 721 AH) and others. Some of his students were Ibn al-Khaṭīb (d. 776 AH), Ibn Al-Khashshāb (d. 774 AH) and Ibn al-Shudayyid (d. c. 776 AH).

Ibn Juzayy was the author of a number of works, many of which are lost today. The most famous of those that are available in print today are the following:

1. *Al-Tashīl li 'Ulūm al-Tanzīl* – a commentary on the Qur'ān.
2. *Taqrīb al-Wuṣūl ilā 'Ilm al-Uṣūl* – on the principles of Islamic jurisprudence (Islamic legal theory).
3. *Al-Qawānīn al-Fiqhiyya* - on comparative jurisprudence.

Author's Preface

In the Name of God, Most Gracious, Most Merciful

Peace and blessings be upon Our Master Muḥammad, and upon all his family and companions.

The expert jurist, scholar, legist, versatile exegete, exemplar, adviser, leader and noble and pure vizier, Abū l-Qāsim, son of the eminent jurist, noble and pure vizier, Abū Ja'far Aḥmad, son of the jurist scholar and noble and pure vizier, Aḥmad ibn Abū l-Qāsim Al-Kalbī (may God be pleased with him) said:

Praise be to God Who guided us to faith and taught us the Qur'ān; peace and blessings be on our master, who called us towards the best of religions and who was sent to man and jinn, and upon all his family and companions and those who follow them in goodness.

This is a book in which we have mentioned religious beliefs that must be held by all Muslims, and for which we have established definitive logical evidences, which we derived from the traditional transmitted sciences, and which we acquired from the chosen radiances. In these we adopted what is found in the Book and the Sunna, and we paid tribute to the way of the pious predecessors of this community.

The objective for our penning of this book was threefold, which will prove extremely useful to those whom God guides:

* **The First Objective**: To mention the evidences and proofs for religious beliefs, so that the person who reads these can advance from (the level of mere) imitation to (the level of) certain knowledge.

* **The Second Objective**: For those evidences or most of them to be taken from the Qur'ān, as it is God's supreme proof and His firm rope, and to show that the Qur'ān contains the knowledge of the earlier and later ones.

* **The Third Objective:** We have only talked about the main issues that the Sharīa has mentioned and that were discussed by the early predecessors, and we have ignored the various controversies and debates that occurred after them. We omitted those matters that were the cause of disagreement amongst the various sects, so that the person who acquires (an understanding of) this book can tread the clear path and adhere to the firm handhold.

This book contains three fundamentals and a final word:

- The First Fundamental is with respect to Divine Matters.
- The Second Fundamental is with respect to Prophets, Rulers, Leaders and Companions.
- The Third Fundamental is with respect to the Hereafter.
- The Final Word contains useful advice in line with the book's objective.

The First Fundamental
Divine Matters

Section One

Establishing the Existence of God, Most High, and that He is the Lord of the Worlds and the Creator of all Creation

Know that the evidences for God's existence, may He be glorified, are innumerable and immeasurable, for everything indicates and points towards Him.

Let us summarize the discussion on this in three ways:

- **The First Way: Inference from the signs that He has placed in the various things that exist.**

These consist of the earth, the heavens, animals, plants, mountains, oceans, winds, rains, the sun, the moon, night, day and other creations, all of which indicate that they have a Maker Who made them and a Creator Who invented them.

This is the meaning contained in the following verses:

- "People, worship your Lord, who created you and those before you." [Al-Baqara 21][1]
- "In the creation of the heavens and earth ... there are signs in all these for those who use their minds." [Al-Baqara 164][2]

---

[1] "People, worship your Lord, who created you and those before you, so that you may be mindful [of Him]; who spread out the earth for you and built the sky; who sent water down from it and with that water produced things for your sustenance. Do not, knowing this, set up rivals to God." Qur'ān 2:21-22

[2] "In the creation of the heavens and earth; in the alternation of night and day; in the ships that sail the seas with goods for people; in the water which God sends down from the sky to give life to the earth when it has been barren, scattering all kinds of creatures over it; in the changing of the winds and clouds that run their appointed courses between the sky and earth: there are signs in all these for those who use their minds." Qur'ān 2:164

- "One of His signs is that He created you from dust" [Al-Rūm 20-25][3]
- "Did We not make the earth smooth ... and luxuriant gardens?" [Al-Naba' 6-16][4]

All mention of things in existence in the Qur'ān give this same meaning and this occurs very frequently in the Qur'ān.

Look – may Allah guide you – at what is closest to you, which is your own self; in it you will see wondrous workmanship and a marvellous arrangement that hold decisive proof. For this reason, God has mentioned His creation of man in numerous places:

- "We created man from an essence of clay," until the verse, "then you will die." [Al-Mu'minūn 12-15][5]

---

[3] "One of His signs is that He created you from dust and- lo and behold!- you became human and scattered far and wide. Another of His signs is that He created spouses from among yourselves for you to live with in tranquillity: He ordained love and kindness between you. There truly are signs in this for those who reflect. Another of His signs is the creation of the heavens and earth, and the diversity of your languages and colours. There truly are signs in this for those who know. Among His signs are your sleep, by night and by day, and your seeking His bounty. There truly are signs in this for those who can hear. Among His signs, too, are that He shows you the lightning that terrifies and inspires hope; that He sends water down from the sky to restore the earth to life after death. There truly are signs in this for those who use their reason. Among His signs, too, is the fact that the heavens and the earth stand firm by His command. In the end, you will all emerge when He calls you from the earth." Qur'ān 30:20-25

[4] "Did We not make the earth smooth, and make the mountains to keep it stable? Did We not create you in pairs, give you sleep for rest, the night as a cover, and the day for your livelihood? Did We not build seven strong [heavens] above you, and make a blazing lamp? Did We not send water pouring down from the clouds to bring forth with it grain, plants, and luxuriant gardens?" Qur'ān 78:6-16

[5] "We created man from an essence of clay, then We placed him as a drop of fluid in a safe place, then We made that drop into a clinging form, and We made that form into a lump of flesh, and We made that lump into bones, and We clothed those bones with flesh, and later We made him into other forms––glory be to God, the best of creators!–– then you will die." Qur'ān 23:12-15

- "And in yourselves too, do you not see?" [Al-Dhāriyāt 21][6]

How amazing is the arrangement of man's creation from a despicable fluid, the formation of his bones and veins of various types - each one with its own specialized function, the permeation of nutrition to each limb proportionately, the various abilities created within him, his being specifically blessed with intellect that differentiates him from animals, how he sees with his eyes, listens with his ears, speaks with his tongue, holds with his hands and all the other wonders that will never cease even if they are to be considered for a significant length of time. There is therefore no doubt that there has to be a Planner Who planned this and a Creator Who perfected this.

Then look again, and you will see in the universe things that are much larger than man, such as the sky, the earth etc. These things contain a majestic form and amazing wisdoms that cannot be fathomed.

God has mentioned this in the verses:

- "Which is harder to create: you people or the sky that He built," until the verse, "and setting firm mountains [in it] for you and your animals to enjoy?" [Al-Nāziʿāt 27-33][7]
- "The creation of the heavens and earth is greater by far than the creation of mankind..." [Ghāfir 57]

Then look at every small or big thing, whether living or not, and the subtleties of wisdom and planning will become apparent to you. Everything that you see or hear of is decisive proof, independently indicating to the existence of its Creator. How great is God's evidence! How many signs are there that point to Him!

---

[6] Qurʾān 51:21

[7] "Which is harder to create: you people or the sky that He built, raising it high and perfecting it, giving darkness to its night and bringing out its morning brightness, and the earth, too, He spread out, bringing waters and pastures out of it, and setting firm mountains [in it] for you and your animals to enjoy?" Qurʾān: 27-33

Here, three questions may be posed:

* **The First Question:** What is the evidence that these things that exist were created after having been non-existent?

The **response** to this is that the evidence is based on two approaches:

- **The First Approach:** The attributes of these things change by their movements, stillness and other contingencies that occur to them. This negates their possessing the attribute of being eternal and affirms their having come into being after non-existence.

This line of reasoning was used by the Prophet Abraham (peace be with him) as mentioned by God in the Qurān in the verse:

- "When the night grew dark over him he saw a star and said, 'This is my Lord,' but when it set, he said, 'I do not like things that set,'" until the verse, "I have turned my face as a true believer towards Him who created the heavens and the earth." [Al-Anām 76-79][8]

When Abraham saw the star, the moon and the sun set and change their status he realized that they were created and he used this as evidence for their creator. This occurred when he was still a child prior to becoming an adult. Another view is that he only said this to illustrate this point to his people and refute their belief.[9]

- **The Second Approach** is that every person knows that he himself came into being after having been non-existent and he sees this in others as well. God Almighty said:

---

[8] "When the night grew dark over him he saw a star and said, 'This is my Lord,' but when it set, he said, 'I do not like things that set.' And when he saw the moon rising he said, 'This is my Lord,' but when it too set, he said, 'If my Lord does not guide me, I shall be one of those who go astray.' Then he saw the sun rising and cried, 'This is my Lord! This is greater.' But when the sun set, he said, 'My people, I disown all that you worship beside God. I have turned my face as a true believer towards Him who created the heavens and the earth.'" Qurān 6:76-79

[9] The second view has been preferred by the author himself in his exegesis of the Qurān. (*Al-Tashīl* p. 259)

- "Was there not a period of time when man was nothing to speak of?" [Al-Insān 1][10]
- "I created you, though you were nothing before." [Maryam 9][11]

Likewise, he sees that the plants come into being after having been non-existent. God Almighty said:

- "You sometimes see the earth lifeless, yet when We send down water it stirs and swells and produces every kind of joyous growth" [Al-Ḥajj 5][12]

* **The Second Question:** What is the evidence that these things that are created need a creator and that they do not create themselves?

The **response** to this is based on three approaches:

- **The First Approach** is that it is impossible for a thing to create itself because the creator must come before the thing created and a thing cannot come before itself. God mentioned the fallaciousness of such a claim in the verse:
  - "Were they created without any agent? Were they the creators?" [Al-Ṭūr 35][13]

Consider the example of your own self. You did not know about yourself before it came into being. How then is it possible for you to be its creator? In this regard, God Almighty said:

- "I did not make them witnesses to the creation of the heavens and earth, nor to their own creation" [Al-Kahf 51][14]

- **The Second Approach** is that all things that are made are of two types: One type is what human beings are capable of (making), such as a book, a building etc. The other type is what human beings are not capable of

[10] Qur'ān 76:1
[11] Qur'ān 19:9
[12] Qur'ān 22:5
[13] Qur'ān 52:35
[14] Qur'ān 18:51

making, such as forming a human being out of water, taking out a fruit from a stick etc. There is no doubt that the first type requires a maker, for when you see a book, you know for certain that it must have an author; and when you see a house that is built, you know for certain that its walls and roof did not form themselves.

Likewise, the second type also indicates to its maker out of necessity. In fact, the indication here is stronger because the workmanship is more astounding, and the marks of wisdom are more apparent. God Almighty said:

- "You will not see any flaw in what the Lord of Mercy creates. Look again! Can you see any flaw? Look again! And again! Your sight will turn back to you, weak and defeated." [Al-Mulk 3-4][15]
- "Do they not see the sky above them--how We have built and adorned it, with no rifts in it?" [Qāf 6][16]

- **The Third Approach** is that it is logically possible for the universe to exist and it is also possible for it not to exist. The fact that it is in existence indicates that there must be someone who gave preference to (the possibility of) its existence over (that of) its non-existence. God Almighty said:

- "Your Lord creates what He pleases and chooses what He wills." [Qaṣaṣ 68][17]

* **The Third Question:** What is the evidence that the creator of all things in existence is God Almighty?

The **response** to this is that no one besides Him, may He be glorified, has the ability to make such created things as He has done. The explanation of this is that everything that exists must necessarily be living and rational like

---

[15] Qur'ān 67:3-4
[16] Qur'ān 50:6
[17] Qur'ān 28:68

man, living and irrational like cattle, or inanimate and non-living like the sky, earth, stars, sun, moon, celestial objects and natures etc.

Undoubtedly, a living rational being is not able to form a human being out of water, bring out a fruit from a stick, or do any other type of creation. If a living rational being is unable to do this, it is more likely and probable that a living non-rational being is unable to do so; and if the living is unable to do so then it is more likely and probable that the non-living will not be able to. Thus, it is proven that the creator of all created things is not of their species, but He is greater than them, and this is God, most High.

It is obvious that if all created beings have to come together to create the smallest of created things, such as an ant, they will not be able to do so. If they cannot do this for the smallest thing, then it is more likely and probable that they won't be able to do this for the largest. In this regard, God said:

- "Those you call on beside God could not, even if they combined all their forces, create a fly." [Ḥajj 73][18]

God has mentioned His singularity in creation in the following and other similar verses:

- "Consider [the semen] you eject- do you create it yourselves or are We the Creator?" [Al-Wāqi'a 58-59] until the verse, "so [Prophet] glorify the name of your Lord, the Supreme." [Al-Wāqi'a 74][19]

---

[18] Qur'ān 22:73

[19] "Consider [the semen] you eject – do you create it yourselves or are We the Creator? We ordained death to be among you. Nothing could stop Us if We intended to change you and recreate you in a way unknown to you. You have learned how you were first created: will you not reflect? Consider the seeds you sow in the ground–is it you who make them grow or We? If We wished, We could turn your harvest into chaff and leave you to wail, 'We are burdened with debt; we are bereft.' Consider the water you drink– was it you who brought it down from the rain-cloud or We? If We wanted, We could make it bitter: will you not be thankful? Consider the fire you kindle– is it you who make the wood for it grow or We? We made it a reminder, and useful to those who kindle it, so [Prophet] glorify the name of your Lord, the Supreme." Qur'ān 56:58-74

- "Who is better: God, or those they set up as partners with Him? Who created the heavens and earth?" [Al-Naml 59-60] until the verse, "Say, 'Show me your evidence then, if what you say is true.'" [Al-Naml 64][20]
- "If you ask the disbelievers who created the heavens and earth and who harnessed the sun and moon, they are sure to say, 'God.'" [Al- Ankabūt 61][21]

- **The Second Way: Inference from the Reports of the Prophets**

Know that the prophets – peace be on them – called the creation to believe in God. Miracles appeared at their hands, the like of which ordinary human beings could not perform such as bringing out a she-camel from a rock, turning a staff into a snake, bringing the dead to life, the splitting of the moon, water gushing from between the fingers and other such feats that evidenced their truthfulness. Thus, it became necessary to believe in the deity that they called towards and to accept what they reported.

Thereafter, some people accepted them and some rejected them. Those who rejected them were destroyed in various ways that only God, most High, is capable of doing, as God, most High, said:

---

[20] "Say [Prophet], 'Praise be to God and peace on the servants He has chosen. Who is better: God, or those they set up as partners with Him? Who created the heavens and earth? Who sends down water from the sky for you– with which We cause gardens of delight to grow: you have no power to make the trees grow in them– is it another god beside God? No! But they are people who take others to be equal with God. Who is it that made the earth a stable place to live? Who made rivers flow through it? Who set immovable mountains on it and created a barrier between the fresh and salt water? Is it another god beside God? No! But most of them do not know. Who is it that answers the distressed when they call upon Him? Who removes their suffering? Who makes you successors in the earth? Is it another god beside God? Little notice you take! Who is it that guides you through the darkness on land and sea? Who sends the winds as heralds of good news before His mercy? Is it another god beside God? God is far above the partners they put beside him! Who is it that creates life and reproduces it? Who is it that gives you provision from the heavens and earth? Is it another god beside God?' Say, 'Show me your evidence then, if what you say is true.'" Qur'ān 27:59-64

[21] Qur'ān 29:61

- "Some We struck with a violent storm; some were overcome by a sudden blast; some We made the earth swallow; and some We drowned." [Al-ʿAnkabūt 40][22]

The prophets and those who had accepted them were saved, as God, most High said:

- "In the end, We shall save Our messengers and the believers." [Yūnus 103][23]

This was evidence for the validity of what they said and of the lordship of the One they called towards. God has mentioned this in the following verse and in other incidents of the previous communities:

- "If they reject you [Prophet], so did the people of Noah before them, and those of Ad, Thamud, Abraham, Lot, Midian. Moses too was called a liar. I gave the disbelievers time, but in the end I punished them. How I condemned them!" [Ḥajj 42-44][24]

All the reports of the prophets - peace be on them - that appear in the Qurān convey the same meaning, and this is replete in the Qur'ān.

Question: If it is said that the reports of the prophets are only known through the information provided by the lawgiver, then how can this be evidence against a person who denies the sacred law?

The **response** to this is based on two approaches:

- **The First Approach** is that the miracles of the prophets and the destruction of those who rejected them are known from the sacred law and from other sources. These were epic events that were evident. God, most High, mentioned them in the Qur'ān as well in the other scriptures that He revealed, and they were extensively transmitted by communities of the people of the scripture, sages, historians, poets and others.

---

[22] Qur'ān 29:40
[23] Qur'ān 10:103
[24] Qur'ān 22:42-44

Also, their remnants bear testimony to this, as God Almighty said:

- "Say, 'Travel throughout the earth and see what fate befell those who rejected the truth.'" [Al-Anʿām 11][25]
- "[Remember] the tribes of Ad and Thamud: their history is made clear to you by [what is left of] their dwelling places." [Al-ʿAnkabūt 38][26]
- "These disbelievers must have passed by the town that was destroyed by the terrible rain--did they not see it?" [Al-Furqān 40][27]

Thus, the argument is established against those who deny the sacred law as well those who do not deny it.

- **The Second Approach:** We will establish definitive evidence for the truthfulness of the lawgiver with respect to the information he provides. Thus, it will be necessary to accept the reports of the prophets and our inference will prove to be valid.

- The Third Way: The existence of God Almighty is attested to by sound disposition

This is also intuitively evidenced in the mind. Every person finds within himself the need for servitude and senses that he is under the supremacy of lordship. As a result, he realizes with certainty that this great kingdom must have a Grand King and that this perfect system must have a Wise Planner. God Almighty said:

- "So [Prophet] as a man of pure faith, stand firm and true in your devotion to the religion. This is the natural disposition[28] God instilled in mankind." [Al-Rūm 30][29]

---

[25] Qurʾān 6:11
[26] Qurʾān 29:38
[27] Qurʾān 25:40
[28] The natural disposition refers to the sound disposition with which God created people in terms of their readiness to recognize and accept the truth, to reject falsehood and distinguish between right and wrong.
[29] Qurʾān 30:30

The Messenger of God (may God bless him and give him peace) said: "Every child is born with the natural disposition."

This meaning is indicated in the following Qur'ānic verse:

- "[Prophet], when your Lord took out the offspring from the loins of the Children of Adam and made them bear witness about themselves, He said, 'Am I not your Lord?' and they replied, 'Yes!'" [Al-A'rāf 172][30]

Due to the fact that souls were naturally created with the disposition to recognize God, the messengers (may God's blessings be on them) said to their people: "Can there be any doubt about God, the Creator of the heavens and earth?" [Ibrāhīm 10][31]

Even if anyone forgets this at the time of prosperity he must return to it at the time of difficulty as God Almighty said:

- "And if harm afflicts the people, they call out sincerely to their Lord." [Al-Rūm 33][32]
- "Say [Prophet], 'Who is it that saves you from the dark depths of land and sea when you humbly and secretly call to Him.'" [Al-An'ām 63][33]

---

[30] "[Prophet], when your Lord took out the offspring from the loins of the Children of Adam and made them bear witness about themselves, He said, 'Am I not your Lord?' and they replied, 'Yes, we bear witness.' So you cannot say on the Day of Resurrection, 'We were not aware of this.'" Qur'ān 7:172

[31] Qur'ān 14:10

[32] Qur'ān 30:33

[33] Qur'ān 6:63

Section Two
Monotheism
The Meaning of 'There is no god but God'

Know that God is One God, there is no god besides Him, He has no partner, He has no rival, He has no child, He has no parent, and He has no spouse. God Almighty said:

- "Say, 'He is God the One'" [Al-Ikhlāṣ 1][34] until the end of the *sūra*.

The evidence of His Oneness, may He be Glorified, is based on several approaches, which the Qur'ān has shown, and there can be no better explanation than that of God in establishing monotheism:

* **The First Approach** is that everything created is created by one creator, because a single act cannot proceed from two doers. Thus, it is established that the creator is one, and this is God Almighty.

In this regard, God Almighty said:

- "Yet the disbelievers take as their gods things beneath Him that create nothing, and are themselves created." [Furqān 3][35]
- "Say, 'Consider those "partners" of yours that you call upon beside God. Show me! What part of the earth did they create? What share of the heavens do they possess?'" [Fāṭir 40][36]
- "All this is God's creation. Now, show Me what your other gods have created." [Luqmān 11][37]

---

[34] "Say, 'He is God the One, God the eternal. He begot no one nor was He begotten. No one is comparable to Him.'" Qur'ān 112:1-4

[35] Qur'ān 25: 3

[36] Qur'ān 35: 40

[37] Qur'ān 31: 11

*** The Second Approach** is that evidence indicates that everything that exists besides God Almighty is created and originated and that it is God Who created it. A created thing cannot be a partner, counterpart or equivalent of its creator, because it is His slave. He created it when He wished and He can destroy it when He wishes.

In this regard, God Almighty said:

- "Those you call upon instead of God are created beings like you." [Al-A'rāf 194][38]
- "Say, 'Should I seek a Lord other than God, when He is the Lord of all things?'" [Al-An'ām 164][39]

*** The Third Approach** is that if we are to assume that there are two gods, and one of them wills for a certain person to die whilst the other wills for him to live; or if one of them wills to move an object and the other wills to keep it still, then there can only be one of three situations:

- The will of both of them is accomplished. This is impossible because the same person cannot be dead and alive (at the same time), and there cannot be motion and stillness (of an object) together.
- The will of neither of them is accomplished, which implies that both of them are incompetent and inadequate. This is also impossible because a person has to be either alive or dead, and an object has to be either in motion or still.
- The will of one of them is accomplished and not the other. In such case, the one whose will is accomplished is the god and the other one whose will is not accomplished is not a god, because he was overcome and subdued.

[38] Qur'ān 7:194

[39] Qur'ān 6:164

Thus, it is established that God is one. This is the meaning of the verses:

- "If there had been in the heavens or earth any gods but Him, both heavens and earth would be in ruins." [Al-Anbiyā' 22][40]
- "Say, 'If there were other gods along with Him, as they say there are, then they would have tried to find a way to the Lord of the Throne.'" [Al-Isrā' 42][41]

* **The Fourth Approach** is that if we have to assume that there are two gods who are creators, each one of them will assume autonomy over the things He created as opposed to the other, and the things created by one of them will be distinct from the things created by the other. However, we see that all created things are linked to one another and they subsist in a perfect arrangement and plan. This indicates that their creator, controller and owner is one, who is God Almighty.

The explanation of all created things being linked to one another is that man and all other animals feed off the vegetation produced by the earth. This vegetation is nourished by the rain that falls from the sky when the winds blow and stir the clouds. The sun and the moon travel in their orbit in a specific arrangement and they serve many purposes such as the ripening of fruit, alternation of day and night, change of the seasons and defining the years and the months. So, consider the correlation between animals, vegetation, the sky, the earth, clouds, winds, the sun, the moon, the night and the day and it will become clear to you that all of those things are subjugated by the power of the One, the All Powerful.

A further exposition of this is that it is not acceptable for there to be two kings with authority in one city. Since the universe is similar to a single city in terms of its organization and the correlation of its parts to one another, it is not possible for it to have but one lord, who is God Almighty. This is the meaning of the verse:

---

[40] Qur'ān 21:22
[41] Qur'ān 17:42

- "God has not taken a son, nor is there with Him any god. If it were so, then every god would have taken what He created and they would have tried to overtake each other." [Al-Mu'minūn 91][42]

- **In Response to the Christians**

Know that Jesus, son of Mary – May God bless Muḥammad and him – is one of God's servants and messengers. God created him in the womb of his mother, the virtuous Mary, without a father. Miracles were displayed at his hands indicating the legitimacy of his prophethood and mission. These are mentioned by God in the Qur'ān, such as his speaking in the cradle, bringing the dead back to life etc. All of these occurred with God's permission and power.

The Christians exaggerated with respect to his status and committed atrocious disbelief that was logically unacceptable and religiously objectionable. God Almighty called them to retract from their disbelief and falsehood when He said to them:

- "People of the Book, do not go to excess in your religion, and do not say anything about God except the truth: the Messiah, Jesus, son of Mary, was nothing more than a messenger of God, His word, directed to Mary, a spirit from Him." [Al-Nisā' 171][43] until the verse, "The Messiah would never disdain to be a servant of God, nor would the angels who are close to Him." [Al-Nisā' 172][44]

The Prophet (may God bless him and give peace) invited them to a prayer duel but they refused as they knew that they were not following the truth and

---

[42] Qur'ān 23:91
[43] "People of the Book, do not go to excess in your religion, and do not say anything about God except the truth: the Messiah, Jesus, son of Mary, was nothing more than a messenger of God, His word, directed to Mary, a spirit from Him. So, believe in God and His messengers and do not speak of a 'Trinity'- stop [this], that is better for you- God is only one God, He is far above having a son, everything in the heavens and earth belongs to Him and He is the best one to trust." Qur'ān 4:171
[44] Qur'ān 4:172

they feared that the punishment will come down on them. Some of them, whom God guided, accepted Islam such as the Negus and others.

The statements of the Christians with respect to Jesus (peace be upon him) differed because they had no knowledge of the actual facts and nor did they have any evidence that could be relied on. They took their corrupt religion from people who were not reliable and they based it on lies, dreams and incorrect matters. It was for this reason that God labelled them as being 'astray'.

Some of them claimed that "Jesus is God's son", as God mentioned about them in the verse:

- "They have asserted, 'God has a child.'" [Al-Baqara 116][45]

Some of them claimed that God is Jesus himself, as God related about them in the verse:

- "Those who say, 'God is the Messiah, the son of Mary,' are defying the truth." [Al-Māida 17][46]

Some of them professed the Trinity, as God Almighty said:

- "Those people who say that God is the third of three are defying [the truth]" [Al-Māida 73][47]

God is far above all these claims of theirs.

The evidence for the falsity of their claim that "Jesus is God's son" is based on four approaches.

* **The First Approach** is that God has the ability to create a child without a father, just as He was able to create Adam without a mother or father. This is the meaning of the verse:

---

[45] Qurān 2:116
[46] Qurān 5:17
[47] Qurān 5:73

- "In God's eyes Jesus is just like Adam: He created him from dust, said to him, 'Be', and he was." [Āl-ʿImrān 59][48]

*** The Second Approach** is that a child has to be of the same species of its parent and a wife must be of the same species as that of her husband. God Almighty - there is nothing like unto Him. Jesus and his mother were from the human species. This proves that God has no child or spouse.

This is the meaning of the verse:

- "The Messiah, son of Mary, was only a messenger; other messengers had come and gone before him; his mother was a virtuous woman; both ate food [like other mortals]." [Al-Māʾida 75][49]

*** The Third Approach** is that a spouse and child are only taken when there is a need for them. It is not correct to assert that God Almighty has a need for anything else and thus He does not take any child or spouse.

This is the meaning of the verse:

- "They say, 'God has children!' May He be exalted! He is the Self-Sufficient One; everything in the heavens and the earth belongs to Him." [Yūnus 68][50]

*** The Fourth Approach** is that everything that exists besides God Almighty is other than Him, because He created it and gave it existence. It therefore cannot be His child. God Almighty says:

- "It does not befit the Lord of Mercy [to have offspring]: there is no one in the heavens or earth who will not come to the Lord of Mercy as a servant." [Maryam 92-93][51]

---

[48] Qurʾān 3:59
[49] Qurʾān 5:75
[50] Qurʾān 10:68
[51] Qurʾān 19:92-93

As for the claim of those Christians who say that, "God is the Messiah son of Mary" this is disproved based on four approaches:

- **The First** is that the Messiah used to worship God.

- **The Second** is that he used to sleep, eat and drink, become hungry and thirsty and was subject to human issues, all of which are not possible for God Almighty.

- **The Third** is that they claimed that he was crucified and killed. This contradicts their claim that, "He is God" because God is living and does not die. They falsely claimed that, "Jesus was crucified and killed." This was something they acquired from the fabrications of the Jews. God Almighty said:

- "They did not kill him, nor did they crucify him, though it was made to appear like that to them." [Al-Nisāʾ 157][52]
- "God said, 'Jesus, I will take you back and raise you up to Me.'" [Āl-ʿImrān 55][53]

Thereafter, based on their false claim of crucifixion, they instituted the worship of the cross. It is thus clear that their religion is an untruth, based on an untruth, which is based on another untruth. Jesus will come down to earth and destroy the cross.

- **The Fourth** is that Jesus was a child and later became an adult. God Almighty is free of this.

As for those of them who claim that, "God is the third of three," their claim is invalidated based on three approaches:

- **The First** is the previously mentioned evidences of God's Oneness and the impossibility of there being two gods.

- **The Second** is that both Jesus and Mary used to worship God, offer prayers and fast. If they had been gods, they would not have worshipped

[52] Qurʾān 4:157
[53] Qurʾān 3:55

another being. Jesus himself acknowledged that God was his Lord. God Almighty said about him:

- "The Messiah himself said, 'Children of Israel, worship God, my Lord and your Lord.'" [Al-Māida 72][54] This is also found in the Gospel that they have in their possession.

- **The Third** is that both Jesus and Mary were subject to human issues, which do not apply to a god.

- **In Response to Idol Worshippers**

The evidence for the invalidity of their religion is based on four approaches:

- **The First** is that idols are created things as these people themselves made them with their own hands. A created thing cannot be a god. It was for this reason that Abraham (peace be upon him) reproached them by saying:

- "He said, 'How can you worship things you carve with your own hands, when it is God who has created you and all your handiwork?'" [Al-Ṣāffāt 95-96][55]

- **The Second** is that they do not possess the attributes of divinity such as life, knowledge, power etc. Therefore, Abraham said to his father:

- "Father, why do you worship something that can neither hear nor see nor benefit you in any way?" [Maryam 42][56]

God Almighty said:

- "Say, 'Consider those you invoke beside Him: if God wished to harm me, could they undo that harm? If God wished to show me mercy, could they withhold that mercy?'" [Al-Zumar 38][57]

---

[54] Qur'ān 5:72
[55] Qur'ān 37:95-96
[56] Qur'ān 19:42
[57] Qur'ān 39:38

- **The Third** is that they are subject to ruin and degradation. Don't you see how Abraham broke them into pieces to use that as proof against his people!

At the time of the conquest of Makka, the Messenger of God (may God bless him and give him peace) entered the city whilst there were idols fastened with lead around the Sacred House. The Prophet (may God bless him and give him peace) began pointing to those idols with a stick he was holding whilst saying: "The truth has come, and falsehood has passed away: falsehood is bound to pass away."[58] As soon as he pointed to any of those idols directly, it fell backward, until there was not a single idol left standing.

- **The Fourth** is the previously mentioned evidences for God's Oneness.

- **In Response to the Magi**

In respect of their claim that goodness comes from light and evil comes from darkness and in response to those who worship the fire, the sun and the like.

The evidence for the falsehood of their claim is based on two approaches:

- **The First** is the previously mentioned evidences for God's Oneness.

- **The Second** is that the sun, moon, stars, light, darkness etc. all contain features of being made and evidences of being created. Consider the inference of Abraham that they were not gods based on their setting. Also, consider the changes that occur to them such as eclipses etc. and this will show you that they are created and in need. Anything that is like this cannot be a god nor can it give effect to any occurrence.

God Almighty said:

- "Praise belongs to God who created the heavens and the earth and made darkness and light; yet the disbelievers set up equals to their Lord!" [Al-Anʿām 1][59]

---

[58] As he was instructed to say in Qurʾān 17:81.

[59] Qurʾān 6:1

- "Do not bow down in worship to the sun or the moon, but bow down to God who created them, if it is truly Him that you worship." [Fuṣṣilat 37][60]

Notwithstanding the above, their statement is an empty claim void of any evidence.

- **In Response to Those Who Believe in the Force of Nature**

The evidence for the falsehood of their claim is based on two approaches:

- **The First** is that nature does not possess the attribute of life, power or will and therefore no act can be attributed to it.

- **The Second** is that the difference in things is evidence that nature does not have any effect, as it can only produce one type of thing. Consider the verses:

- "Have you not considered how God sends water down from the sky and that We produce with it fruits of varied colours?" [Fāṭir 27][61]
- "...all watered with the same water, yet We make some of them taste better than others." [Al-Raʿd 4][62]

---

[60] Qurʾān 41:37

[61] Qurʾān 35:27

[62] Qurʾān 13:4

Section Three
Establishing God's Attributes

Know that God, may He be glorified, is living and does not die. He is the First before everything and the Last Who will remain after everything else perishes. He has knowledge of everything and He knows what is secret and what is even more hidden. "Nothing on earth or in heaven is hidden from Him." [Āl- 'Imrān 5][63] He exercises His will over all things in existence and "carries out whatever He wills." [Hūd 107][64] Nothing in the universe occurs but by His decree, determination and will. What He has willed occurs and what He has not willed does not occur. He has power over everything. He speaks, hears and sees. He hears everything and sees everything.

The evidence for the establishment of these attributes is based on three approaches:

* **The First Approach** is that these are attributes of perfection and grandeur and their opposites are attributes of deficiency such as inability and ignorance. God Almighty cannot be described with defects and it is thus necessary to describe him with their opposites.

Consider the verse, "They attribute to God what they themselves dislike." [Al-Naḥl 62][65] Thus, God Almighty is free of any attribute of imperfection that a person dislikes for himself and He is described with the most exalted attributes.

---

[63] Qur'ān 3:5
[64] Qur'ān 11:107
[65] Qur'ān 16:62

* **The Second Approach** is that these attributes are mentioned in the sacred sources and therefore must be believed in.

God Almighty says about His attribute of **Life**:

- "Put your trust in the Living [God] who never dies." [Al-Furqān 58] [66]

He said about (His attribute of) **Knowledge**:

- "God has full knowledge of everything." [Al-Baqara 282] [67]

He said about (His attribute of) **Will**:

- "Your Lord carries out whatever He wills." [Hūd 107] [68]

He said about (His attribute of) **Power**:

- "God has power over all things." [Al-Baqara 284] [69]

He said about (His attribute of) **Speech**:

- "To Moses God spoke directly." [Al-Nisā᾿ 164] [70]

He said about (His attributes of) **Hearing** and **Sight**:

- "God is all hearing, all seeing." [Al-Ḥajj 75] [71]

God has been described with these attributes in many places in the Qur᾿ān.

---

[66] Qur᾿ān 25:58
[67] Qur᾿ān 2:282
[68] Qur᾿ān 11:107
[69] Qur᾿ān 2:284
[70] Qur᾿ān 4:164
[71] Qur᾿ān 22:75

* **The Third Approach** is to infer each attribute from its specific evidence.

This is based on the fact that all things that are made by Him – may He be glorified – have been made perfectly and all created things are precise in form, as God Almighty said, "...Who gave everything its perfect form."[Al-Sajda 7] [72]

Thus, His accomplishment in respect of created things, His organization of the universe and His protection of the earth and the heavens are evidence of His Life. God Almighty said, "The Living, the All-Sustaining." [Al-Baqara 255] [73] The meaning of the Arabic word *Qayyūm* (translated as the All-Sustaining) is the Being Who takes charge of everything in terms of power and grasp.

His creation of these things is evidence of His Power. God Almighty says drawing attention to this:

- "It is He who creates human beings from fluid, then makes them kin by blood and marriage: your Lord is all powerful!" [Al-Furqān 54][74]
- "Control of the heavens and earth belongs to Him; He gives life and death; He has power over all things." [Al-Ḥadīd 2] [75]

His mastery and perfection of them is indicative of His Knowledge and Sight. God Almighty said:

- "How could He who created not know His own creation?" [Al-Mulk 14] [76]

His allocation of various forms and times to them is evidence of His Will. God Almighty said:

- "He grants female offspring to whoever He will, male to whoever He will." [Al-Shūrā 49] [77]

---

[72] Qur'ān 32:7
[73] Qur'ān 2:255
[74] Qur'ān 25:54
[75] Qur'ān 57:2
[76] Qur'ān 67:14
[77] "God has control of the heavens and the earth; He creates whatever He will- He grants female offspring to whoever He will, male to whoever He will, or both male

- "Your Lord creates what He pleases and chooses those He will." [Al-Qaṣaṣ 68][78]

His revelation of scriptures and His commandments and prohibitions is indicative of His Speech. God Almighty said:

- "Grant it to him so that he may hear the word of God." [Al-Tawba 6][79]

His response to supplication is evidence of His Hearing. God Almighty said:

- "Who is it that answers the distressed when they call upon Him?" [Al-Naml 62][80]

Note:

God has the most beautiful names and sublime attributes, which He used to describe himself and which the Messenger of God (may God bless him and give him peace) described Him with.

God Almighty said: "The Most Excellent Names belong to God: use them to call on Him." [Al-A'rāf 180][81]

The Prophet (may God bless him and give him peace) said: "God has ninety-nine names and whoever enumerates[82] them will enter Paradise."[83]

---

and female, and He makes whoever He will barren: He is all knowing and all powerful." Qur'ān 42:49-50

[78] Qur'ān 28:68

[79] "If any one of the idolaters should seek your protection [Prophet], grant it to him so that he may hear the word of God, then take him to a place safe for him, for they are people with no knowledge [of it]." Qur'ān 9:6

[80] Qur'ān 27:62

[81] Qur'ān 7:180

[82] 'Enumerates them' means to learn them, believe in them, ponder over their meanings, worship God by them, supplicate with them, and act by them according to one's belief in them.

[83] Ṣaḥīḥ Al-Bukhāri – Book 50 Ḥadīth 894

Section Four
Transcendence of God Almighty

Know that God, may He be glorified, possesses supreme majesty and absolute perfection and that He is free from any defect and absolved of any imperfection. This is the meaning of the Arabic phrase "*Subḥānallah*" (often translated as "Glory be to God.")

He is not subject to inability or failure. God Almighty said:

- "God is not to be frustrated by anything in the heavens or on the earth." [Fāṭir 44][84]
- "We created the heavens, the earth, and everything between, in six Days without tiring." [Qāf 38][85]

He is not subject to heedlessness and He does not sleep. God Almighty said:

- "Neither slumber nor sleep overtakes Him." [Al-Baqara 255][86]

Error and forgetfulness do not apply to Him. God Almighty said:

- "My Lord does not err or forget." [Ṭāhā 52][87]

He is just in all His rulings and actions and is never oppressive or unfair.

Every blessing of His is grace and every punishment of His is justice. This is because He is the owner of everything and an owner can do what He wills with his possessions and deal with His servants as He wishes. God Almighty said:

- "He cannot be called to account for anything He does, whereas they will be called to account." [Al-Anbiyā̓ 23][88]

---

[84] Qur̓ān 35:44
[85] Qur̓ān 50:38
[86] Qur̓ān 2:255
[87] Qur̓ān 20:52
[88] Qur̓ān 21:23

He, most High, does not resemble anything. God Almighty said:

- "There is nothing like unto Him." [Al-Shūrā 11][89]
- "Can He who creates be compared to one who cannot create? Why do you not take heed?" [Al-Naḥl 17][90]

- **A Note and Advice:**

Know that the Qur'ān and the prophetic traditions contain certain words that apparently give the impression of resemblance, such as the verse: "established on the throne" [Ṭāhā 5][91], the prophetic tradition about 'descent'[92] and other such texts. It is necessary for the servant to believe in these without giving (God any) resemblance and without divesting (God of His attributes) or interpretation. He must entrust the knowledge of this to God Almighty Himself and say, "I believe in what God Almighty has said and what His Messenger (may God bless him and give him peace) has told us, in the meaning intended by God and His Messenger (may God bless him and give him peace); and God and His Messenger know best."

---

[89] Qur'ān 42:11
[90] Qur'ān 16:17
[91] Qur'ān 20:5
[92] This refers to a tradition in Bukhārī and Muslim that reads as follows:
Our Lord descends to the heaven during the last third of every night, and He says: "Who is calling upon me that I may answer him? Who is asking from me that I may give him? Who is seeking My forgiveness that I may forgive him?"

This is the way of submission that leads to safety, for which God praised those who possessed this attribute when He said:

- "Those firmly grounded in knowledge say, 'We believe in it: it is all from our Lord'" [Āl-ʿImrān 59][93]

This was the position of the companions and successors as well the leaders of the Muslims such as Al-Shāfiʿī, Aḥmad ibn Ḥanbal, Sufyān, Ibn al-Mubārak and others who are to be followed and whose way should be adopted.[94]

---

[93] Qurʾān 3:7

[94] Later scholars were compelled by circumstance to resort to figurative interpretation (*taʾwīl*) that preserved the divine transcendence and that was within the parameters of classical Arabic usage without claiming that the interpretation suggested was the intended meaning with certainty.

For example, with respect to the Qurʾānic phrase, *"yad Allāh"* (the literal translation of which is "the hand of God"), the approach of the earlier scholars, such as those mentioned by the author, was to confirm and believe in it without knowing its meaning. Instead they consigned the knowledge of what is meant to God. This is called *tafwīḍ*. Later scholars interpreted 'hand' to refer, for example, to the assistance or power of Allah. This is called figurative interpretation (*taʾwīl.*)

Both these approaches have been accepted amongst the Ahl al-Sunna as mentioned by Imām al-Nawawī in his commentary on Ṣaḥīḥ Muslim and other scholars.

The Second Fundamental
Prophets, Angels, Rulers and Companions

Section One
Establishing Prophethood

Know that God Almighty dispatched prophets and sent messengers to the creation. He revealed to them scriptures and gave them eminence over all people. He gave preference to some of them over others. Some of them have been mentioned by God in the Qur'ān and some have not been mentioned. The first of them was Adam, the father of mankind and the last of them was Muḥammad - may God bless and give him and all of them peace.

The evidence for their truthfulness in their claim of prophethood was the extraordinary miracles that appeared at their hands. God Almighty said, "We sent Our messengers with clear signs." [Al-Ḥadīd 25][95] The Prophet (may God bless him and give him peace) said, "There was no prophet but that he was given signs, the like of which people believed in."[96]

Know that in the sending of prophets there were several wisdoms:

* **The First Wisdom** is that people are of different intellects and divergent views. Therefore, God sent the prophets (peace be upon them) to clarify the disagreements between people. God Almighty said:

- "Mankind was a single community, then God sent prophets to bring good news and warning, and with them He sent the Scripture with the Truth, to judge between people in their disagreements." [Al-Baqara 213][97]

* **The Second Wisdom** is that God created the creation to worship Him and He laid down certain rules for them consisting of instructions and prohibitions, which they have to adhere to. He made the prophets intermediaries between Him and His servants to convey to them the rules He laid down. If God had not sent the prophets, the creation would have been

[95] Qur'ān 57:25
[96] Ṣaḥīḥ al-Bukhārī
[97] Qur'ān 2:213

lost, they would not have known how to worship God and they would not have known what to do and what not to do. God Almighty said: "We send messengers only to give good news and to warn." [Al-Anʿām 48][98]

For this reason, God made it binding on His creation to obey the messengers and He said, "All the messengers We sent were meant to be obeyed, by God's leave." [Al-Nisāʾ 64][99]

* **The Third Wisdom** is that God Almighty sent the prophets to establish proof against the creation and to remove their excuses. God Almighty said:

- "Nor do We punish until We have sent a messenger." [Al-Isrāʾ 15][100]
- "They were messengers bearing good news and warning, so that mankind would have no excuse before God, once the messengers had been sent." [Al-Nisāʾ165][101]

For this reason, God will say in the hereafter, "Company of jinn and mankind! Did messengers not come from among you to recite My revelations to you and warn that you would meet this Day?" [Al-Anʿām 130][102]

---

[98] Qurʾān 6:48
[99] Qurʾān 4:64
[100] Qurʾān 17:15
[101] Qurʾān 4:165
[102] Qurʾān 6:130

Section Two
Establishing the Prophethood of the Seal of the Prophets, Leader of the Messengers, Best of the Earlier and Later Ones, Mercy to the Worlds, Abū l-Qāsim Muḥammad ibn ʿAbdullāh ibn ʿAbd al-Muṭṭalib ibn Hāshim, the Unlettered, Arab, Qurashī Prophet (may God's salutations be on him and may He bless him and give him peace, mercy, honour and dignity)

Know that God Almighty sent him to all of mankind, Arabs and non-Arabs, and to the *jinn.* He made it binding on everyone to enter into his religion, which is the religion of Islam, other than which God does not accept. By his creed, He abrogated all other creeds. By his sacred law, He sealed all sacred laws. God Almighty said:

- "People, I am the Messenger of God to you all." [Al-Aʿrāf 158][103]
- "If anyone seeks a religion other than [Islam] complete devotion to God, it will not be accepted from him." [Āl-ʿImrān 85][104]
- "But he is God's Messenger and the seal of the prophets." [Al-Aḥzāb 40][105]

There are many evidences that point towards the validity of His mission and His prophethood. Let us group these into five categories:

---

[103] Qurʾān 7:158
[104] Qurʾān 3:85
[105] Qurʾān 33:40

The First Category The Noble Qur'ān that God Almighty revealed to him. "Though it is an unassailable Scripture, which falsehood cannot touch from any angle, a Revelation sent down from the Wise One, Worthy of All Praise." [Fuṣṣilat 41-42] [106]

The Qur'ān proves the validity of his prophethood (May God bless him and give him peace) in ten ways:

* **The First** is its eloquence and purity of style that distinguishes it from all other speech. This was acknowledged by the Arabs who heard it. Likewise, its amazing arrangement in terms of the endings of its verses and the beauty of its compilation. Some scholars have regarded its arrangement as an additional indication over and above its eloquence.

* **The Second** is that the Prophet (may God bless him and give him peace) called on the creation to produce something similar to it, but they were unable to do so, and they failed to produce anything, despite their zeal to oppose it and their eagerness to falsify it, and notwithstanding the eloquence of the Arabs in that era. Had they been able to do any of that, they would have done so and they would not have conceded to being killed and imprisoned and to their children and wealth being captured.

This was evidence that it was beyond the capacity of human beings. God Almighty said:

- "If you have doubts about the revelation We have sent down to Our servant, then produce a single *sūra* like it- enlist whatever supporters you have other than God- if you truly [think you can]." [Al-Baqara 23] [107]

[106] Qur'ān 41:41-43
[107] Qur'ān 2:23

God Almighty stated that they will not be able to do so in the verse:

- "Say, 'Even if all mankind and jinn came together to produce something like this Qur'ān, they could not produce anything like it, however much they helped each other.'" [Al-Isrā' 88][108]

* **The Third** are the incidents of the former communities and the stories of the prophets and others that it narrated, which it could not have known except by revelation from God Almighty as God, may He be glorified said:

- "These accounts are part of what was beyond your knowledge [Muhammad]. We revealed them to you. Neither you nor your people knew them before now." [Hūd 49][109]

* **The Fourth** is what it mentioned about unseen events that had not yet occurred and thereafter occurred exactly as it had predicted, such as the following verses among others:

- "... to make it prevail over all religions." [Al-Tawba 33][110]
- "... you will most certainly enter the Sacred Mosque." [Al-Fatḥ 27][111]

Similarly, what it mentioned about the secrets of people and what they kept hidden within their hearts such as the following verses among others:

- "... (they) say inwardly." [Al-Mujādila 8][112]

---

[108] Qur'ān 17:88
[109] Qur'ān 11:49
[110] "It is He who has sent His Messenger with guidance and the religion of truth, to make it prevail over all [other] religions, however much the idolaters may hate this." Qur'ān 9:33
[111] "God has truly fulfilled His Messenger's vision: 'God willing, you will most certainly enter the Sacred Mosque in safety, shaven-headed or with cropped hair, without fear!'- God knew what you did not- and He has granted you a speedy triumph." Qur'ān 48:27
[112] "Have you not seen how those who have been forbidden to hold secret conversations go back afterwards and hold them, and conspire with one another in what is sinful, hostile, and disobedient to the Messenger? When they come to you they greet you with words God has never used to greet you, and say inwardly, 'Why

- "... (they) distort the meaning." [Al-Nisā' 46][113]

*** The Fifth** is the knowledge of religious beliefs that it contains, such as the names and attributes of God Almighty and the states of the hereafter, its providing evidence for the same and its repudiation of various communities with definitive arguments and other such matters, which the intellect is incapable of grasping and which can only be established by revelation from God Almighty.

*** The Sixth** are the rulings that are instituted therein, the exposition of the lawful and unlawful that it contains and the noble character traits that it directs towards, in which the goodness of this world and the hereafter are combined.

*** The Seventh** is its being protected from replacement and change, unlike other scriptures as God Almighty said, "We have sent down the Qur'ān Ourself, and We Ourself will guard it." [Al-Ḥijr 9][114]

*** The Eighth** is its having been made easy to remember - which is something that is clearly known through first-hand experience. God Almighty said, "We have made the Qur'ān easy to remember. But is there any rememberer there?" [Al-Qamar 17][115]

*** The Ninth** is that anyone who recites or listens to it does not become tired or bored despite its frequent repetition.

*** The Tenth** are the incantations and invocations that it contains, which provide a cure for sickness and disorders, as has been recorded in the

---

does God not punish us for what we say?' Hell will be punishment enough for them: they will burn there- an evil destination." Qur'ān 58:8

[113] "Some Jews distort the meaning of [revealed] words: they say, 'We hear and disobey,' and 'Listen,' [adding the insult] 'May you not hear,' and 'Raina [Look at us],' twisting it abusively with their tongues so as to disparage religion." Qur'ān 4:46

[114] Qur'ān 15:9

[115] Qur'ān 54:17

prophetic traditions with regard to the Qur'ānic treatment of the person bitten by a scorpion by means of the opening chapter; and the prophetic tradition that the 'recitation of the last part of *Sūra Al-Ḥashr* is a cure from every illness besides death.'

The Second Category The remarkable miracles and clear signs that appeared at his hands (May God bless him and give him peace). There are many indeed. Some scholars have said that they reach up to one thousand miracles. Other scholars have said that, "God did not give any prophet a miracle except that he gave Muḥammad (May God bless him and give him peace) a similar type of miracle that was either better or equal to it."

These included the incidents when the moon split at his instance; when water gushed from between his fingers; when he was able to satiate a large number with a minimal quantity of food; his prediction about many matters of the unseen that later occurred exactly as he said; when pebbles glorified God in his palm; when stones greeted him with peace; when a tree came towards him and testified to his prophethood; when a gazelle and lizard spoke to him and testified to his prophethood; when a donkey and camel spoke to him; when a wolf testified to his prophethood; when a tree stump yearned for him when he left it; when a new-born baby testified to his prophethood; when he restored the eye of Qatāda that had fallen onto his cheek and which then became the better of his two eyes; when God gave life to the dead for his sake; when the dead testified to his apostleship; when God answered his prayer in many matters such as bringing back the sun after it had set; and his prayer to seek the coming and the cessation of rain etc.

Know that the miracles of the Prophet (May God bless him and give him peace) are of two categories:

- The first category includes those that we know definitively, such as the splitting of the moon, because the Qur'ān explicitly mentioned its occurrence, the literal meaning of which cannot be abandoned without any evidence, and it was also reported in authenticated narrations with many chains. Similarly, the gushing of water and increase of food have been reported by reliable and numerous narrators from a vast number of individuals from numerous companions, which occurred on major occasions and in large gatherings.

- The second category are those whose type we know about definitively due to their frequent occurrence although we do not have definitive knowledge about the individual incidents, such as predictions and the answering of prayers since these occurred many times from the Prophet (May God bless him and give him peace) to the extent that we have definitive knowledge of their collective purport although each individual incident is not such. When similar incidents are put together they concur in their import and together they produce a miracle.

The Third Category Inference from the great merits and noble character traits that God Almighty gifted him with, and the beautiful attributes and majestic qualities that He brought together for him, which God Almighty only brings together for the most beloved and most honoured of His servants.

These include his noble lineage, beautiful form, far-reaching intellect, sound understanding, eloquent tongue, powerful senses, abundant knowledge, profuse worship, beautiful character, tolerance, patience, gratitude, abstinence, justice, trustworthiness, honesty, humility, pardon, chastity, generosity, bravery, modesty, dignity, calm, reverence, loyalty, faithfulness, kinship, kindness, sociability, good governance etc.

He (may God bless him and give him peace) possessed all traits of perfection at once, and he encompassed various majestic qualities, reaching therein the highest of ranks and the farthest of goals. This has been transmitted by narrators without any disagreement. This will become apparent to anyone who peruses his biography. The following statement of God Almighty is sufficient in this regard:

- "Truly you have a strong character." [Al-Qalam 4][116]

---

[116] Qur'ān 68:4

Also, consider the narration about Abū Sufyān's conversation with Heraclius, the King of Rome, and his enquiry about his states, character and lineage (may God bless him and give him peace). When Abū Sufyān told him about those things, Heraclius immediately confirmed his prophethood. This is an authentic narration recorded by Al-Bukhārī and others.

ʿAbdullāh ibn Salām said, "When the Messenger of God (may God bless him and give him peace) came to Madīna, I came to look at him. When I saw his face clearly, I recognised that his face was not that of an impostor."

The Fourth Category Inference from the signs that appeared prior to his being granted prophethood. These include the wondrous events that occurred at his birth, such as the light that emerged when he was born, the shaking of Chosroe's palace, the extinguishing of the fire of the Persians etc.

Amongst these is the prayer of Abraham and Ishmael – may God bless him and them – to raise him from amongst their progeny. God Almighty relates this prayer of theirs in the words, "Our Lord, make a messenger of their own rise up from among them." [Al-Baqara 129][117]

Another sign is the protection of his lineage (peace be on him) from every defect such that he descended from the most prestigious lineage and the best of homes. He (may God bless him and give him peace) said, "God selected from amongst mankind Adam..."[118] ʿAlī ibn Abī Ṭālib (may God be pleased with them) said, "There was never any adultery in our lineage, it was only marriage."[119]

God warded off the army of the elephant from Makka and destroyed it for his sake (peace be on him.) God Almighty said:

- "Did you [Prophet] not see how your Lord dealt with the army of the elephant?" [Al-Fīl 1][120]

[117] Qurʾān 2:129
[118] Recorded by Al-Ḥākim in Al-Mustadrak (3/83)
[119] Mentioned by Qāḍī ʿIyāḍ in Al-Shifāʾ (1/119)
[120] Qurʾān 105:1

Another sign is the reference made to his prophethood by Moses, Jesus and all the other prophets. God Almighty said:

- "God took a pledge from the prophets, saying, 'If, after I have bestowed Scripture and wisdom upon you, a messenger comes confirming what you have been given, you must believe in him and support him...'" [Āl-ʿImrān 3:81][121]

Another sign is the mention of him found in the Torah and the Gospel. God Almighty said:

- "Those who follow the Messenger- the unlettered prophet they find described in the Torah that is with them, and in the Gospel." [Al-Aʿrāf 157][122]

Another sign is the sky's being guarded with flames and the devils' being prevented from eavesdropping ever since his prophethood, as stated by God Almighty relating the words of the Jinn,

- "We used to sit in places there..." [Al-Jinn 9][123]

Amongst these signs are the successive reports from monks, rabbis and scholars of the people of the book about his description, the description of his community, his name and his signs, such as his being recognized by Baḥīra, the monk, when he was a child; the knowledge about him that Zayd ibn ʿAmr ibn Nufayl, Waraqa ibn Nawfal and other scholars of the former religious scriptures possessed; the mention of him found in the poetry of the earlier monotheists such as Tubbaʿ, Aws ibn Ḥāritha and others; and the mention of him that God made fortune tellers, such as Shiqq, Saṭīḥ, Khunāfir, Sawād and others, predict.

---

[121] "God took a pledge from the prophets, saying, 'If, after I have bestowed Scripture and wisdom upon you, a messenger comes confirming what you have been given, you must believe in him and support him. Do you affirm this and accept My pledge as binding on you?' They said, 'We do.' He said, 'Then bear witness and I too will bear witness.'" Qurʾān 3:81

[122] Qurʾān 7:157

[123] "We used to sit in places there, listening, but anyone trying to listen now will find a shooting star lying in wait for him." Qurʾān 72:9

❧ **The Fifth Category** ☙ Inference from the signs that appeared after him (may God bless him and give him peace), such as the dominance of his religion over all other religions in confirmation of the statement of God Almighty, "It is He who has sent His Messenger with guidance and the religion of truth, to show that it is above all [other] religions;" [Al-Tawba 33][124] and the conquest of the east and the west by his community in confirmation of the prophetic statement, "The earth was rolled up for me, so I saw its east and its west. The empire of my community will reach as far as it was rolled up for me."[125]

See how his community overpowered the kingdom of Chosroes, Caeser and other kings of the world, whose scourge was eradicated despite the vastness of their kingdom and their numerous armies. No one is able to do this except with the command of God Almighty.

Another sign is the fact that his religion for more than seven hundred years[126] remained dominant in all corners of the globe with its laws protected and without any change to its limits or obscurity of its features.

Another sign is the huge number of his community and his followers and the entrance of people in droves into his religion. No community of any other prophet before him reached such a large number. The Prophet (may God bless him and give him peace) said, "I have hope that I will be the one with the most followers on the day of rising."[127]

Amongst these signs are his blessings of deep knowledge, the understanding of religion, pronouncement of wisdom and consciousness of

---

[124] Qur'ān 9:33

[125] Recorded by Muslim in the Book of Trials and the Signs of the Hour, Chapter on the Destruction of this Community at the Hands of One Another.

[126] The author, who lived in the seventh and eighth century after the *hijra* wrote this in his time. Today, the religion of Islam still remains the fastest growing religion in the world and is expected to outstrip Christianity by the end of the century.

[127] Recorded by Al-Bukhāri in the Book on Adherence to the Book and the Sunna, Chapter on the Statement of the Prophet (may God bless him and give him peace): "I have been sent with the most comprehensive words" and also by Muslim in the Book of Faith, Chapter on the Obligation of Faith in the Mission of Our Prophet Muḥammad (may God bless him and give him peace.)

God Almighty that was apparent in his companions (may God be pleased with them), and other such things that they would not have possessed had it not been for their following of him (may God bless him and give him peace.)

Amongst these signs are the miracles, the answering of prayers and the extraordinary feats that appear at the hands of the righteous ones of his community, all of which indicate towards the truthfulness of their prophet (may God bless him and give him peace) and his honour in the sight of God Almighty.

In Response to the Jews

The Jews denied the prophethood of our prophet (may God bless him and give him peace) out of jealousy and in rejection of the truth. When the evidence of his truthfulness was established by his miracles, they resorted to the denial of abrogation and they claimed that, "The sacred law of Moses (may God bless him and give him peace) cannot be repealed by any other sacred law, as abrogation entails new knowledge coming to light (and thus inconstancy in the divine will), which is impossible for God Almighty."

The response to them is based on seven approaches:

* **The First Approach** is that abrogation does not imply new knowledge coming to light (or inconstancy in the divine will) but it is similar to the case when a master instructs his slave to perform some task, and when he does it to the extent that the master wanted, he instructs him to do another task. There is nothing wrong if God transfers his servants from one sacred law to another, just as He transfers them from one state to another.

Don't you see that a human being is initially a drop of fluid, then a blood-clot, and then he passes thereafter through many states as God Almighty said:

- "We created man from an essence of clay, then We placed him as a drop of fluid in a safe place, then We made that drop into a clinging form, and We made that form into a lump of flesh..." until the verse, "and then, on the Day of Resurrection, you will be raised up again." [Al-Mu'minūn 12-16][128]

The same applies to the stages of plants. God Almighty said:

- "Have you not considered that God sends water down from the sky, guides it along to form springs in the earth, and then, with it, brings forth vegetation of various colours, which later withers, turns yellow before your eyes, and is crumbled to dust at His command?" [Al-Zumar 21][129]

Likewise, is the alternation of night and day, each stage thereof obliterates the one before it. All of this occurs in accordance with the will of God Almighty. "God erases or confirms whatever He wills." [Al-Ra'd 39][130] "He cannot be called to account for anything He does, whereas they will be called to account" [Al-Anbiyā' 23][131]

* **The Second Approach** is that their sacred law had abrogated those before it, since in the era of Adam (may God bless him and give him peace) it was permitted for a man to marry his sister due to the necessity of procreation, and thereafter this was prohibited. Similarly, the observation of Sabbath was not instituted prior to them. So, just as their sacred law could abrogate other laws, other laws can abrogate it.

* **The Third Approach** is that Moses (may God bless him and give him peace) informed his followers of Muḥammad (may God bless him and give him peace) and it became binding on them to accept him. Prior to his being sent

---

[128] "We created man from an essence of clay, then We placed him as a drop of fluid in a safe place, then We made that drop into a clinging form, and We made that form into a lump of flesh, and We made that lump into bones, and We clothed those bones with flesh, and later We made him into other forms--glory be to God, the best of creators!-- then you will die and then, on the Day of Resurrection, you will be raised up again." Qur'ān 23:12-16

[129] Qur'ān 39:21

[130] Qur'ān 13:39

[131] Qur'ān 21:23

they used to inform others about him, as God Almighty said, "They had been praying for victory against the disbelievers." [Al-Baqara 89][132]

Many of them acknowledged this. Some of them accepted Islam such as Abdullāh ibn Salām, Kaʿb al-Aḥbār and others. Some of them were deprived of Islam because of their innate jealousy and their fate of wretchedness. God Almighty said. "Those to whom We gave the Scripture know that this [Quran] is revealed by your Lord [Prophet] with the truth." [Al-Anʿām 114][133]

God reproached them for abandoning faith despite their recognition thereof, when He said, "People of the Book, why do you deny God's revelations when you can see they are true? People of the Book, why do you mix truth with falsehood? Why do you hide the truth when you recognize it?" [Āl-ʿImrān 70-71][134]

*** The Fourth Approach** is that the Islamic creed requires belief in Moses, Jesus, Muḥammad and all the other prophets (may God bless all of them.) The Qurʾān corroborates the Torah and the Gospel. However, the Judaic creed requires belief in certain prophets and not others, as they reject Jesus and Muḥammad (may God bless them both). They had also murdered and denied a number of prophets.

It is well-known that faith in all (prophets) is superior to faith in some of them and denial of others. This is the meaning of the verse:

- "So [you believers], say, 'We believe in God and in what was sent down to us and what was sent down to Abraham, Ishmael, Isaac, Jacob, and the Tribes, and what was given to Moses, Jesus, and all the prophets by their Lord. We make no distinction between any of them, and we devote ourselves to Him.'" [Al-Baqara 136][135]

---

[132] Qurʾān 2:89. In other words, they used to seek victory from God against the polytheists by saying, "O God, help us by the prophet to be sent at the end of time." (*Al Tashīl*)

[133] Qurʾān 6:114

[134] Qurʾān 3:70-71

[135] Qurʾān 2:136

* **The Fifth Approach** is that the followers of all creeds from amongst the Jews, Christians and the Arabs are unanimous in the reverence of Abraham (peace be on him.) The religion of Islam is the religion of Abraham, and therefore it is obligatory on them to follow it. God Almighty said:

- "The faith of your forefather Abraham." [Al-Ḥajj 78][136]
- "People of the Book, why do you argue about Abraham when the Torah and the Gospels were not revealed until after his time?" [Āl-ʿImrān 65][137] until the verse, "Abraham was neither a Jew nor a Christian. He was upright and devoted to God, never an idolater." [Āl-ʿImrān 67][138]

* **The Sixth Approach** is that the people of the book, the Jews and the Christians, had altered and changed their religion and differed therein. They made additions to God's scriptures and deleted things from them. They murdered and rejected the prophets (peace be on them.) They worshipped others besides God and they attributed to Him things that were not appropriate for His majesty and transcendence. They went to the extreme in the disobedience of God, to the extent that God punished them by making some of them into apes and swines.

God then sent Muḥammad (may God bless him and give him peace) to show them the truth about what they differed, bring them back to it in matters they had altered, and to take them out of darkness into light. God said:

- "Truly, this Quran explains to the Children of Israel most of what they differ about." [Al-Naml 76][139]
- "O people of the Scripture, Our messenger has come to you to clarify for you much of what you were hiding from the Scripture, and to pardon over much." [Al-Māʾida 15][140]

---

136 Qurʾān 22:78
137 Qurʾān 3:65
138 Qurʾān 3:67
139 Qurʾān 27:76
140 Qurʾān 5:15

The abovementioned approaches or most of them can also be used in response to the Christians.

*** The Seventh Approach** is the argument that had they been entitled to good-fortune in the hereafter, they would have wished for death to attain this good-fortune. However, they did not wish for it in the past, nor do they presently wish for it. This is evidence of the fallaciousness of their claim.

This is the meaning of the verse:

- "Say [Prophet], 'You who follow the Jewish faith, if you truly claim that out of all people you alone are friends of God, then you should be hoping for death.' But because of what they have stored up for themselves with their own hands they would never hope for death." [Al-Jumuʿa 6-7][141] It is mentioned in the books of Quranic exegesis that had they wished for death, they would have died. Some of the scholars said that this was a miracle of the Prophet (may God bless him and give him peace) that lasted throughout his life (peace be on him.)

Know that there are some Jews who acknowledge the prophethood of Muḥammad (may God bless him and give him peace) but they say that, "He was only sent to the Arabs specifically." This statement is evidently self-contradictory, because if a person acknowledges his prophethood, he is bound to accept everything he says and the Prophet (may God bless him and give him peace) informed us that he was sent to all of mankind. He therefore must be believed in this.

Some of them reject his prophethood because he was an Arab and he was not from the Children of Israel. This is clear ignorance and its invalidity can be proved from many angles.

- One of them is that God selects for His mission whomsoever He wishes from whichever community He will. God Almighty said, "God is fully aware where He makes His message." [Al-Anʿām 124][142]

---

[141] Qurʾān 62:6-7
[142] Qurʾān 6:124

Prophethood is a mercy from God, that He allocates to whomsoever He wills from amongst His servants. God Almighty said, "God chooses for His grace whoever He will." [Al-Baqara 105][143]

- Another is that there were many prophets from amongst the Arabs such as Hūd, Ṣāliḥ and Shuʿayb.
- Another is that, the fact that he (may God bless him and give him peace) was an illiterate Arab is more indicative and glaring in respect of his miracles, as he produced wisdom and knowledge without any previous experience and learning and without prior knowledge of scripture.

[143] Qurʾān 2:105

Section Three

Know that the angels are servants of God Almighty, who are honoured in His sight. They worship and glorify Him. They obey Him and do not disobey Him. God Almighty praised them in His Book by saying:

- "No! They are only His honoured servants," [Al-Anbiyā 26][144] until the verse, "indeed they themselves stand in awe of Him." [Al-Anbiyā 28][145]
- "...and those that are with Him are never too proud to worship Him, nor do they grow weary, they glorify Him tirelessly night and day." [Al-Anbiyā 19-20][146]

Some of them are envoys to the prophets. Some of them are assigned the task of removing souls. Some of them are guardians over human beings. Some of them have other duties. No one is fully aware of them besides God Almighty.

Belief in the angels is obligatory, because God Almighty said:

- "Anyone who does not believe in God, His angels, His Scriptures, His messengers, and the Last Day has gone far, far astray." [Al-Nisā 136][147]

The Prophet (may God bless him and give him peace) mentioned belief (faith) in the narration of Gabriel (peace be on him) and he said, "that you have faith in God, His angels, His scriptures, His messengers, and the Last Day, and you believe in fate, the good and bad of it, the sweet and bitter of it."[148]

---

[144] Qurān 21:26

[145] "No! They are only His honoured servants, they do not speak before He speaks and they act by His command. He knows what is before them and what is behind them, and they cannot intercede without His permission--indeed they themselves stand in awe of Him." Qurān 21:26-28

[146] Qurān 21:19-20

[147] Qurān 4:136

[148] Recorded by Muslim in the Book of Faith, Chapter on the Explanation of Faith (*Īmān*), *Islam*, *Iḥsān* and the Signs of the Hour.

Section Four

Know that Abū Bakr Al-Ṣiddīq, ʿUmar ibn al-Khaṭṭāb, ʿUthmān ibn ʿAffān, and ʿAlī ibn Abi Ṭālib (may God be pleased with them) were just rulers, each one of whom assumed the caliphate being entitled thereto.

The view of the *Ahl al-Sunna*[149] is that they were the best of people after the Messenger of God (may God bless him and give him peace), and that the position of their ranks in virtue is according to the position of their ranks in the caliphate.

As for Abū Bakr Al-Ṣiddīq, the evidence for his leadership is the consensus of the Muslims to put him forward after the Messenger of God (may God bless him and give him peace). The Messenger of God (may God bless him and give him peace) had indicated to his being appointed as the caliph according to what is reported in an authentic narration from Jubayr ibn Muṭʿim about the incident of the woman to whom the Messenger of God (may God bless him and give him peace) said, "If you do not find me, then go to Abū Bakr."[150]

In the narration of ʿĀʾisha (may God be pleased with her), the Prophet (may God bless him and give him peace) said, "God and the Muslims want no one but Abū Bakr."[151]

---

[149] The *Ahl al-Sunna or Ahl al-Sunna wa l-Jamāʿa* literally translates as 'the people of the way and the group' and broadly refers to Muslim orthodoxy and consensus. The 'way' signifies that of the Prophet (may God bless him and give peace) and the 'group' refers to his noble companions (*ṣaḥāba*), and their successors (*tābiʿīn*) and those after them represented by the main spectrum of Muslims in every age.

[150] Muḥammad ibn Jubayr ibn Muṭʿim narrates from his father that a woman asked the Messenger of God for something. He instructed her to come back to him. She said, "O Messenger of God! Tell me, if I come and I don't find you?" My father said, "It was as if she meant death." He said, "If you don't find me, then go to Abū Bakr." Recorded by Al-Bukhāri in the Book of Virtues, Chapter on the Statement of the Prophet (may God bless him and give him peace): "If I had to take a bosom friend." This is also recorded by Muslim in the Book on the Virtues of the Companions, Chapter on the Virtues of Abū Bakr Al-Ṣiddīq (may God be pleased with him).

[151] Recorded by Al-Bukhāri in the Book of the Sick, Chapter on the Statement of the Sick Person: I am in pain. This is also recorded by Muslim in the Book on the Virtues

Umar (may God be pleased with him), was appointed as caliph by Abū Bakr, and the Muslims reached consensus on giving him precedence. The Messenger of God (may God bless him and give him peace) had hinted to his caliphate in an authentic narration reported by Abū Hurayra and ʿAbdullāh ibn ʿUmar. Al-Tirmidhī has recorded from Ḥudhayfa that the Messenger of God (may God bless him and give him peace) said, "Follow the two persons after me: Abū Bakr and ʿUmar."[152]

ʿUthmān (may God be pleased with him), was appointed by the consultative council to whom Umar had delegated the authority to select the caliph. The Muslims reached consensus on his caliphate and thereafter there was an uprising against him by the lay people and they murdered him wrongfully. No one of any significance took part in his murder.

ʿAlī (may God be pleased with him) had sent his two sons, Ḥasan and Ḥusayn (may God be pleased with them), to assist him and guard him. It is reported from Ibn ʿUmar that the Messenger of God (may God bless him and give him peace) mentioned a sedition and said about Uthman, "He will be wrongfully killed in it."[153]

With respect to ʿAlī (may God be pleased with him), there is no doubt that he possessed such noble characteristics and eminent virtues that made him worthy of leadership even with only some of them, such as his close family relationship to the Messenger of God (may God bless him and give him peace), his being his son-in-law, his early entry into Islam, his knowledge, bravery, abstinence etc.

The Muslims reached consensus on appointing him as the caliph after the murder of Uthman and they submitted themselves to his authority.

---

of the Companions, Chapter on the Virtues of Abū Bakr Al-Ṣiddīq (may God be pleased with him).

[152] Recorded by Al-Tirmidhī in his Sunan. Book of Virtues. Chapter on the Virtues of Abū Bakr and ʿUmar.

[153] Recorded by Al-Tirmidhī in his Sunan. Book of Virtues. Chapter on the Virtues of ʿUthmān ibn ʿAffān (may God be pleased with him).

Thereafter, some people opposed him for other reasons. As for the disturbances that occurred thereafter and the discord that arose between ʿAlī and Muʿāwiya, including the companions who sided with each of them, there is no authentic report in that regard. If there is, then silence should be maintained with respect to it and we should refrain from mentioning it. Rather, the best way out should be sought for all of them and they should be spoken of in the best manner. We should hold the best of thoughts about both groups and maintain that despite this, it was ʿAlī who was on the right.

Know that all of the household of the Prophet (may God bless him and give him peace) and all his companions are eminent and righteous individuals. The Noble Qurʾān and authentic reports from the Messenger of God (may God bless him and give him peace) have testified to their virtue. God Almighty said:

- "God wishes to keep uncleanness away from you, people of the [Prophet's] House, and to purify you thoroughly." [Al-Aḥzāb 33][154]
- "Muḥammad is the Messenger of God. Those who follow him are harsh towards the disbelievers and compassionate towards each other." [Al-Fatḥ 29] until the end of the *sūra*.[155]
- "God will be well pleased with the first emigrants and helpers and those who followed them in good deeds, and they will be well pleased with Him." [Al-Tawba 100] until the end of the verse.[156]

---

[154] Qurʾān 33:33

[155] "Muhammad is the Messenger of God. Those who follow him are harsh towards the disbelievers and compassionate towards each other. You see them kneeling and prostrating, seeking God's bounty and His good pleasure: on their faces they bear the marks of their prostrations. This is how they are pictured in the Torah and the Gospel: like a seed that puts forth its shoot, becomes strong, grows thick, and rises on its stem to the delight of its sowers. So God infuriates the disbelievers through them; God promises forgiveness and a great reward to those who believe and do righteous deeds." Qur'an 48:29

[156] "God will be well pleased with the first emigrants and helpers and those who followed them in good deeds, and they will be well pleased with Him: He has prepared Gardens graced with flowing streams for them, there to remain for ever. That is the supreme triumph." Qurʾān 9:100.

The Third Fundamental
The Hereafter

Section One
Establishing the Afterlife

Know that God will bring the dead back to life and gather the creation on the day of rising for reckoning, reward and punishment. The evidence for this is that it is a contingent matter that is not impossible, which has been spoken of by God's scriptures and mentioned by His messengers. It is therefore necessary to believe in it. The mention of it and the details about its states is contained in our sacred law more than in any other.

The evidence that it is a possible occurrence is based on three approaches:

* **The First Approach** is that God Almighty has the ability to restore bodies after their annihilation, just as He was able to create them the first time. God Almighty said:

- "Say, 'He who created them in the first place will give them life again.'" [Yāsīn 79][157]
- "Does man think he will be left alone? Was he not just a drop of spilt-out sperm." [Al-Qiyāma 36-37] until the end of the sūra.[158]
- "He is the One who originates creation and will do it again- this is even easier for Him." [Al-Rūm 27][159]

* **The Second Approach** is that God Almighty had the ability to create the heavens and the earth, which undoubtedly are larger than the creation of man. Likewise, He has the ability to give life to the creation after their death. God Almighty said:

---

[157] Qur'ān 36:79
[158] "Does man think he will be left alone? Was he not just a drop of spilt-out sperm, which became a clinging form, which God shaped in due proportion, fashioning from it the two sexes, male and female? Does He who can do this not have the power to bring the dead back to life?" Qur'ān 75:36-40
[159] Qur'ān 30:27

- "Do the disbelievers not understand that God, who created the heavens and earth and did not tire in doing so, has the power to bring the dead back to life? Yes indeed!" [Al-Aḥqāf 33][160]

*** The Third Approach** is that God Almighty gives life to the earth by the rain after its death. He causes crops to grow therein after there was nothing. In the same way, He will give life to the creation after their death. This is meaning of the statements of God Almighty:

- "You sometimes see the earth lifeless, yet when We send down water it stirs and swells and produces every kind of joyous growth." [Al-Ḥajj 5][161]
- "...how with water We give [new] life to a land that is dead? This is how the dead will emerge [from their graves]." [Qāf 11][162]

Also, consider the statements of God Almighty, drawing attention to His power to gather the creation:

- "The coming of the Hour of Judgement is like the blink of an eye, or even quicker." [Al-Naḥl 77][163]
- "Creating and resurrecting all of you is only like creating or resurrecting a single soul." [Luqmān 28][164]

Know that in the resurrection there are a number of wisdoms:

One of them is that people differ with one another. Therefore, God will resurrect them to establish the truth and decide between them in respect of what they differ. God Almighty said:

- "[Prophet], it is your Lord who will judge between them on the Day of Resurrection concerning their differences." [Al-Sajda 25][165]

---

160 Qur'ān 46:33
161 Qur'ān 22:5
162 Qur'ān 50:11
163 Qur'ān 16:77
164 Qur'ān 31:28
165 Qur'ān 32:25

- "...in order to make clear for them what they have differed about and so that the disbelievers may realize that what they said was false." [Al-Naḥl 39][166]

Another wisdom is that some people are believers whilst others are disbelievers, some are obedient whilst others are sinners. God will therefore resurrect them to recompense each one for his action. God Almighty said:

- "... so that God may reward each soul as it deserves." [Ibrāhīm 51][167]

Had there been no resurrection and reward in the hereafter there would be no distinction between the righteous ones and the evil ones. In the world, they are the same. In fact, sometimes it may occur that a disbeliever and sinner may be in a better condition in the world. Hence, it is necessary that there be a place where the difference in the recompense of each becomes apparent. This is the meaning of the statement of God Almighty:

- "Did you think We had created you in vain, and that you would not be brought back to Us?" [Al-Mu'minūn 115][168]
- "Do those who commit evil deeds really think that We will deal with them in the same way as those who believe and do righteous deeds, that they will be alike in their living and their dying? How badly they judge!" [Al-Jāthiya 21][169]
- "Should We treat those who submit to Us as We treat those who do evil?" [Al-Qalam 35][170]

---

[166] Qur'ān 16:39
[167] Qur'ān 14:51
[168] Qur'ān 23:115
[169] Qur'ān 45:21
[170] Qur'ān 68:35

Section Two
What Will Occur Before the Day of Rising

Know that there is mention in the sacred law about things that will take place between the time a person dies and the day of rising, and these must be believed in, such as the questioning by the two angels and the punishment in the grave.

There is also mention of things that will occur before the day of rising, which are its portents or signs such as the emergence of the great impostor (Dajjāl), the emergence of Gog and Magog, the emergence of the beast, the rising of the sun from the west etc.

The punishment in the grave is evidenced in the Qurʾān and Sunna. The Qurʾān states: "A terrible punishment engulfed Pharaoh's people; they will be brought before the Fire morning and evening." [Ghāfir 45-46][171]

The reason this verse serves as proof thereof is that it is explicit in reference to punishment before the day of rising. This is because the following portion of the verse states: "On the Day the Hour comes, it will be said, 'Throw Pharaoh's people into the worst torment.'" [Ghāfir 46][172] Thus, the punishment before the day of rising can only be in the grave.

The Sunna contains many authentic narrations in this regard. A large number of companions have narrated traditions from the Prophet (may God bless him and give him peace) about the punishment in the grave and the questioning by the two angels. Amongst them are Abū Saʿīd Al-Khudrī, Abū Ayyūb Al-Anṣāri, ʿĀʾisha, ʿUthmān ibn ʿAffān, Al-Barāʾ ibn ʿĀzib, Asmāʾ bint Abū Bakr, Anas ibn Mālik and Abū Hurayra. These narrations have been recorded by leading scholars of ḥadīth such as Muslim, Al-Bukhāri, Al-Tirmidhī, Abū Dāwūd and Nasāʾī. The pious predecessors have agreed on this and this is the view of the *Ahl Al-Sunna* and the vast majority of Muslims.

---

[171] Qurʾān 40:45-46

[172] Qurʾān 40:46

With respect to the signs of the hour there are many narrations that have been reported by numerous companions. Some of them have also been mentioned in the Qur'ān. God Almighty said:

- "And when the peoples of Gog and Magog are let loose..." [Al-Anbiyā' 96][173]
- "When the verdict is given against them, We shall bring a creature out of the earth, which will tell them..." [Al-Naml 82][174]
- "But on the Day some of your Lord's signs come, no soul will profit from faith if it had none before, or has not already earned some good through its faith." [Al-An'ām 158][175] - This will occur when the sun rises from the west at which time the door of repentance will be shut. Prior to this, repentance will be accepted if it validly fulfils all its requirements.

[173] Qur'ān 21:96
[174] Qur'ān 27:82
[175] Qur'ān 6:158

Section Three
The Day of Rising and its States

Know that the sacred law has mentioned things that will take place on the day of rising, and these must be believed in, such as the bridge, the balance, reckoning, retaliation, reading of the books of deeds, the pool of the Prophet (may God bless him and give him peace) and his intercession, and the testimony of the limbs.

The Bridge (or the path over Hell) is evidenced by the Qur'ān in the verse, "lead them all to the path of Hell." [Al-Ṣāffāt 23][176] and by the Sunna in many reports from the Prophet (may God bless him and give him peace) by a number of companions such as Abū Hurayra, Ḥudhayfa, 'Ā'isha, Abū Sa'īd Al-Khudrī, Al-Mughīra ibn Shu'ba as recorded by Muslim, Al-Tirmidhī, Abū Bakr ibn Abī Shayba and other leading scholars of ḥadīth and agreed to by the predecessors and the *Ahl Al-Sunna* of the later generations.

The Balance (or the scale) is evidenced in the Qur'ān in numerous verses such as, "We will set up scales of justice for the Day of Resurrection." [Al-Anbiyā' 47][177] and the verse, "On that Day the weighing of deeds will be true and just." [Al-A'rāf 8][178] as well as in the Sunna by reports from the Prophet (may God bless him and give him peace) by a number of individuals including 'Ā'isha and Anas ibn Mālik as recorded by the scholars of ḥadīth.

The Reckoning is evidenced in the Qur'ān in numerous verses, such as those that describe the day of rising as the day of reckoning, the verse, "He will have an easy reckoning" [Al-Inshiqāq 8][179] and the verse, "By your Lord, We will question them all about their deeds." [Al-Ḥijr 92-93][180] In the Sunna, there are numerous reports from the Prophet (may God bless him and give him peace)

---

[176] Qur'ān 37:23
[177] Qur'ān 21:47
[178] Qur'ān 7:8
[179] Qur'ān 84:8
[180] Qur'ān 15:92-93

by a number of companions including ʿĀʾisha, ʿAbdullāh ibn Masʿūd, Abū Barza Al-Aslamī, ʿAbdullāh ibn ʿUmar and others as recorded by the scholars of ḥadīth and agreed to by the Muslims.

Retaliation is evidenced in the Qurʾān in the verse, "Fair judgement will be given between them." [Zumar 69][181] and in the Sunna by reports from the Prophet (may God bless him and give him peace) by a number of individuals including Abū Hurayra, Abū Saʿīd Al-Khudrī and Anas ibn Mālik as recorded by the scholars of ḥadīth and agreed to by the Muslims.

The Reading of the Book (of Deeds) is evidenced in the Qurʾān in numerous verses such as, "We have bound each human being's destiny to his neck. On the Day of Resurrection, We shall bring out a record for each of them, which they will find spread wide open" [Al-Isrāʾ 13][182] and the verse, "Anyone who is given his Record in his right hand..." [Al-Ḥāqqa 19][183] and in the Sunna by reports from the Prophet (may God bless him and give him peace) by a number of individuals including Abdullāh ibn ʿAmr ibn Al-ʿĀṣ, Abū Mūsā Al-Ashʿarī and Anas ibn Mālik as recorded by the scholars of ḥadīth and agreed to by the Muslims.

The Pool is the *Al-Kawthar* that God has given His prophet (may God bless him and give him peace) as mentioned by God Almighty: "We have truly given *Al-Kawthar* to you [Prophet]," [Al-Kawthar 108] [184] according to the interpretation reported from the Prophet (may God bless him and give him peace) in an authentic narration. This is also evidenced in many reports from the Messenger of God (may God bless him and give him peace) by a number of individuals including Thawbān, Abū Dharr, Anas, ʿĀʾisha, ʿAbdullāh ibn ʿAmr ibn Al-ʿĀṣ, Umm Salama, Abū Hurayra, Sahl ibn Saʿd, ʿUmar ibn Al-Khaṭṭāb, Jābir

---

[181] Qurʾān 39:69

[182] Qurʾān 17:13

[183] "Anyone who is given his Record in his right hand will say, 'Here is my Record, read it." Qurʾān 69:19

[184] Qurʾān 108:1

ibn 'Abdullāh, Ḥudhayfa ibn Al-Yamān, Abū Barza Al-Aslamī and others, as recorded by the scholars of ḥadīth.

The Intercession is evidenced in the Qur'ān in the statement of God Almighty to His messenger, "so that your Lord may raise you to a [highly] praised status" [Al-Isrā' 79][185] and in the Sunna by reports from the Prophet (may God bless him and give him peace) by a number of individuals including Ḥudhayfa, Abū Hurayra, 'Abdullāh ibn 'Umar, Anas ibn Mālik, Jābir ibn 'Abdullāh, Abū Umāma, Abū Mūsā Al-Ash'arī, 'Imrān ibn Al-Huṣayn and others, as recorded by the scholars of ḥadīth and agreed to by the pious predecessors and the *Ahl Al-Sunna.*

The Testimony of the Limbs is evidenced in the Qur'ān in the statement of God Almighty, "On the Day when their own tongues, hands, and feet will testify against them about what they have done" [Al-Nūr 24][186] and the verse, "their ears, eyes, and skins will testify against them for their misdeeds." [Fuṣṣilat 20][187]

It is also evidenced in the Sunna by reports from the Prophet (may God bless him and give him peace) by Anas ibn Mālik, Abū Umāma Al-Bāhilī and others as recorded by the scholars of ḥadīth (may God be pleased with them.)

Know that description of these things that will occur on the day of rising and prior to it and the details of their circumstances have been mentioned in numerous traditions. We have omitted these for the sake of brevity because our intent is only to prove their occurrence and nothing else.

---

[185] Qur'ān 17:79

[186] Qur'ān 24:24

[187] Qur'ān 41:20

Section Four
Paradise and Hell-Fire

Know that God Almighty has made paradise the home of comfort and reward, and He has made hell-fire the home of punishment and retribution. Paradise will be entered by the people of good-fortune, who are the believers, and therein they will be given various types of comforts in the form of food, drink, women, servants, clothing, palaces and other things as mentioned in the Qur'ān in numerous places.

Amongst these are the statements of God Almighty:

- "For those who fear [the time when they will] stand before their Lord there are two gardens," [Al-Raḥmān 46][188] until the end of the *sūra*.
- "...and reward them, for their steadfastness, with a Garden and silken robes," [Al-Insān 12][189] until the end of the description of paradise therein; and other verses.

There are also many authentic reports from the Prophet (may God bless him and give him peace) by a large number of companions in respect of the description thereof.

Know that the people of paradise will see God Almighty. This is evidenced by the statement of God Almighty,

- "On that Day there will be radiant faces, looking towards their Lord." [Al-Qiyāma 22-23][190]

In this context, there have been numerous authentic and explicit reports from the Prophet (may God bless him and give him peace) by a number of companions including Abū Hurayra, Jarīr ibn ʿAbdullāh Al-Bujalī, Suhayb, Ibn ʿUmar, Abū Saʿīd Al-Khudrī and others as recorded by the scholars of ḥadīth.

---

[188] Qur'ān 55:46
[189] Qur'ān 76:12
[190] Qur'ān 75:22-23

Know that the comfort of paradise is perpetual and will never end. This is evidenced in the Qurʾān in the verses:

- "...and there they will remain forever" [Al-Nisāʾ 57][191];
- "...nor will they ever be expelled therefrom" [Al-Ḥijr 48][192] and;
- "...they will taste death no more" [Al-Dukhān 46][193]

There are also numerous reports in this context. The Muslims have reached consensus on this. May God, through His grace and mercy, make us of its inhabitants.

Hell-fire will be entered into by the disbelievers and sinners and they will be punished therein with various forms of punishment as mentioned in the Qurʾān in numerous places such as:

- "Hell lies in wait," [Al-Nabaʾ 21] until the verse, "a fitting requital." [Al-Nabaʾ 26][194];
- "We have prepared a Fire for the wrongdoers that will envelop them from all sides." [Al-Kahf 29][195] and other such verses.

There are also numerous reports that have been recorded in respect of the description thereof.

The disbelievers will necessarily enter into it and will be made to live therein forever with no end. This is evidenced in the Qurʾān in the verses:

---

[191] Qurʾān 4:57

[192] Qurʾān 15:48

[193] Qurʾān 44:46

[194] "Hell lies in wait, a home for oppressors to stay in for a long, long time, where they will taste no coolness nor drink except one that is scalding and dark-- a fitting requital." Qurʾān 78:21-26

[195] "We have prepared a Fire for the wrongdoers that will envelop them from all sides. If they call for relief, they will be relieved with water like molten metal, scalding their faces. What a terrible drink! What a painful resting place!" Qurʾān 18:29

- "But those who reject the truth will stay in Hellfire, where they will neither be finished off by death, nor be relieved from Hell's torment." [Fāṭir 36][196]
- "They will not be brought out of the Fire on that Day, nor will they be given the chance to make amends." [Al-Jāthiya 35][197]
- "those who disbelieve and deny Our messages shall be the inhabitants of the Fire, and there they will remain forever." [Al-Baqara 39][198] and other such verses.

There is also evidence for the same in the Sunna in numerous authentic report and the Muslims have reached consensus on this.

As for the sinning believers, some of them will be pardoned by God Almighty and He will not enter them into the fire. This is evidenced by the verse:

- "God does not forgive the joining of partners with Him: anything less than that He forgives to whoever He will." [Al-Nisā' 48][199] and all mention in the Qur'ān of God Almighty's being described as a lord of mercy, pardon and forgiveness.

In this regard, numerous prophetic reports have also been recorded.

Some of them will be taken to task by God for their sins and He will enter them into the fire and thereafter remove them from it by God's mercy and the intercession of the Prophet (may God bless him and give him peace) and enter them into paradise.

Know that a believer will not be made to remain forever in the fire. The evidence for this from the Qur'ān is the statement of God Almighty, "Whoever has done an atom's-weight of good will see it," [Al-Zalzala 7][200] This is because

---

196 Qur'ān 35:36
197 Qur'ān 45:35
198 Qur'ān 2:39
199 Qur'ān 4:48
200 Qur'ān 99:7

if he is made to remain in the fire forever, he will not obtain reward for his faith and the good actions that he did. Further evidence is the verse, "anything less than that He forgives to whoever He will." [Al-Nisā' 48][201]

In the Sunna, there are numerous traditions in this regard, reported from the Prophet (may God bless him and give him peace) by a number of companions including Abū Hurayra, Abū Saʿīd Al-Khudrī, Jābir ibn ʿAbdullāh, Anas, Ḥudhayfa and ʿImrān ibn Al-Ḥuṣayn, as recorded by the scholars of ḥadīth. This is the view of the *Ahl Al-Sunna* and any Qurʾānic verse or prophetic report that indicates otherwise must be interpreted (to be consistent with this.)

---

201 Qurʾān 4:48

Final Word

Know that faith is the basis of all good acts and it is a prerequisite for the acceptance of all righteous deeds. The rectification of belief is the most stressed of all obligations that God has imposed on His servants. Hence, you must be serious and work hard in this regard.

Here, I offer some advice to you to strengthen your conviction and - God willing - make your religion firm, and I caution you against that which will make your heart waver and corrupt your thinking and intellect.

I advise you to do four things:

* **The First** is to recite the Grand Qur'ān, ponder deeply over its verses and comprehend its meanings, for this is what will illuminate hearts and broaden chests. God Almighty said, "This Quran does indeed show the straightest way." [Al-Isrā' 9][202] God Almighty called it guidance, mercy, a light, a cure, an exposition, glad-tidings and means of insight.

The Messenger of God (may God bless him and give him peace) said that it is, "the Book of God, in which there is news of those who came before you, information about what will happen after you have gone, rulings concerning matters between you. It is the decisive word and is not something to be taken lightly. If any overweening person abandons it, God will crush him, and if anyone seeks guidance elsewhere, God will lead him astray. It is the strong rope of God, it is the wise reminder, it is the straight path, it is that by which desires do not swerve nor do tongues become confused, and the scholars are satiated from it. It does not become worn out by abundant repetition and its wonders do not come to an end. It is that which prompted the *Jinn*, when they heard it, to say, 'Indeed, we have heard a wondrous Qur'ān that gives guidance to the right path, and we have come to believe it.' [Al-Jinn 1-2][203] Whoever speaks in accordance with it proves truthful, whoever acts in accordance with

---

[202] Qur'ān 17:9
[203] Qur'ān 72:1-2

it will be rewarded, whoever judges according to it will be just, and whoever calls towards it will be guided to the straight path."[204]

* **The Second** is to read the traditions of the Messenger of God (may God bless him and give him peace), study his biography, comprehend his speech, and follow his way, for you will come across amazing and wonderful things in his beautiful actions and wise statements that will guide you those who possess intelligence.

God Almighty said:

- "By the star when it sets! Your companion has not strayed; he is not deluded; he does not speak from his own desire." [Al-Najm 1-3][205]
- "Say, 'If you love God, follow me, and God will love you and forgive you your sins.'" [Āl-ʿImrān 31][206]

The Prophet (may God bless him and give him peace) said, "I have left you with two things that as long as you hold firm to, you will not go astray: The Book of God and my way."[207]

* **The Third** is to become acquainted with the reports of the predecessors from amongst the companions and those who came after them, to emulate them and to abandon innovated matters. The Messenger of God (may God bless him and give him peace) said, "My companions are like the stars. Whichever one of them you emulate you will be guided."[208] The Prophet (may God bless him and give him peace), when asked about the saved sect, said,

---

[204] Recorded by Al-Tirmidhī in his Sunan, Book on the Virtues of the Qurʾān, Chapter on what has been mentioned about the virtue of the Qurʾān.
[205] Qurʾān 53:1-3
[206] Qurʾān 3:31
[207] Recorded by Imām Mālik in the Muwaṭṭaʾ, Book of Predestination, Chapter on the Prohibition of the Denial of Fate.
[208] This is narrated by Ibn Abd Al-Barr in his book, the Compendium of the Exposition and Virtue of Knowledge, although the expert scholars of ḥadīth have not authenticated it.

"Those that follow what I and my companions adopt."[209] The Prophet (may God bless him and give him peace) also said, "Beware of innovated things, for they are misguidance. Any of you who comes across that must stick to my way and the way of the rightly guided successors after me. Bite onto it with your back teeth!"[210]

* **The Fourth** is mindfulness of God Almighty, perseverance in acts of obedience, avoidance of sins and bad deeds, because this will increase the light of insight, just as the opposite will put a cover over the heart. God Almighty said:

- "But God gives more guidance to those who are guided." [Maryam 76][211]
- "If you remain mindful of God, He will give you a criterion [to tell right from wrong] and wipe out your bad deeds." [Al-Anfāl 29][212]

He said regarding the converse:

- "No indeed! Their hearts are encrusted with what they have done." [Al-Muṭaffifīn 14][213]
- "Do not yield to those whose hearts We have made heedless of Our remembrance." [Al-Kahf 28][214]

---

[209] Recorded by Al-Tirmidhī in the Book of Faith, Chapter on what has been mentioned regarding the split of this community.
[210] Recorded by Al-Tirmidhī in his Sunan. Book of Knowledge, Chapter on what has been mentioned about Sunna and the Avoidance of Innovations.
[211] Qur'ān 19:76
[212] Qur'ān 8:29
[213] Qur'ān 83:14
[214] Qur'ān 18:28

I caution you against two things:

* **The First** is to become involved in ancient un-Islamic sciences such as philosophy and astronomy, because these generally weaken one's faith, cause the heart to become dark and creates a dislike in the hearts of the believers towards the person who becomes involved in them. This is coupled with the fact that they are sciences that have no benefit and that were not taught by the prophets and messengers. If God knew that there was benefit in these, He would have sent the messengers with them. ʿUmar had instructed that their books be thrown into the sea and he said, "If there is any good in them, then that which He guided us to is better than them."

* **The Second** is to look into obscure matters, to become involved in suspicion and scepticism and to recount the opposing views of the disbelievers and innovators, for this will cause doubt to enter the heart and will shake the pillars of one's conviction. It is for this reason that the lawgiver instructed us to refrain from certain matters and prohibited us from excessive questioning and prying. The Messenger of God (may God bless him and give him peace) said, "Those before you were ruined because of their excessive questions and disagreement with their prophets."[215]

ʿUmar had disciplined a person who asked such questions. The pious predecessors and the Imams always frowned upon such talk. Imam Mālik removed the person who had asked him about *istiwāʾ* saying, "Asking about this is an innovation, and it seems that you are an evil man." Much has been reported from Imam Al-Shāfiʿī and Imam Aḥmad ibn Ḥanbal with regard to their being strict about this.

If it is argued that this is needed in order to respond to those who are in opposition and to refute their statements.

The response to this is that those who oppose us are of two types: disbelievers and innovators.

---

[215] Agreed upon

- As for the disbelievers, the Qurʾān has already refuted their statements and it has showed their deviation and misguidance. It is God's argument against His creation and therefore there is no need for anything else to go with it.

- As for the innovators, their statements should not be related and nor should their arguments be mentioned unless there is a need to do so, in which case a person may become involved in responding to them, just as ʿAlī and Ibn ʿAbbās (may God be pleased with them) responded to the Kharijites when their matter became widespread.

This is what prompted the leading theologians like Abū l-Ḥasan Al-Ashʿarī and Abū Bakr ibn Al-Ṭayyib (may God have mercy on them) to speak on this, due to the advent of the various sects of innovators in their era.

In our time, God has relieved us of their burden because they do not exist, especially in our lands in the Maghreb and the Andalus. Hence, their views should not be given any attention and should not cross the heart or ears of anyone because it is harmful without any benefit. This is because the benefit that it had of deterring them is of no use in their absence, and the harm that it contains such as commission of the prohibition, opposition of the predecessors and the darkening of the heart is present and will affect the person who becomes involved in it.

If it is said that sometimes thoughts may cross one's heart and Satan may insinuate and cast reservations into a person's chest, then what should such a person do?

The answer is that this is a disease, whose cure is clearly found in the Qurʾān and Sunna, in four things:

* **The First** is to seek God's protection from Satan and ignore such thoughts. God Almighty said, "If Satan should prompt you to do something, seek refuge with God- He is all hearing, all knowing." [Al-Aʿrāf 200][216]

[216] Qurʾān 7:200

The Messenger of God (may God bless him and give him peace) said, "Whoever experiences any such thing should say, 'I believe in God,'" and in one narration he said, "He should seek God's protection and refrain."

* **The Second** is the remembrance of God. God, may He be glorified said, "those who have faith and whose hearts find peace in the remembrance of God- truly it is in the remembrance of God that hearts find peace." [Al-Raʿd 28][217]

* **The Third** is to reflect over the evidences and recount the proofs. God Almighty said, "those who are aware of God think of Him when Satan prompts them to do something and immediately they can see [straight];" [Al-Aʿrāf 201][218]

* **The Fourth** is to enquire from an orthodox scholar. God Almighty said, "Ask those who have knowledge if you do not know." [Al-Naḥl 43][219]

We have reached the end of what we set out to do by God's grace. Praise be to God, who guided us to this: had God not guided us, we would never have found the way. We ask God, the Supreme Lord of the grand throne to record for us, in lieu of this book, the reward of those who call towards the right and pronounce the truth, to increase our faith and certainty, and to place together with His recognition a clear light in our hearts.

We conclude with salutations to the one who directed us to God and guided us to the worship of God, who is our master and leader, Muḥammad, may God give him on our behalf the best reward that any prophet is given from his community, and may He let us die on his creed, holding firm to his tradition, by His grace and mercy.

---

[217] Qurʾān 13:28
[218] Qurʾān 7:201
[219] Qurʾān 16:43

www.ingramcontent.com/pod-product-compliance
Lightning Source LLC
Chambersburg PA
CBHW062144160726
48282CB00027B/934